INDIAN
RESTAURANT
MENU
RECIPES

INDIAN RESTAURANT MENU RECIPES

~

S O N I A   A L L I S O N

foulsham
LONDON • NEW YORK • TORONTO • SYDNEY

foulsham

The Publishing House
Bennetts Close,
Cippenham, Berks SL1 5AP

ISBN 0-572-01703-0

Typeset in Great Britain by Typesetting Solutions, Slough, Berks.
Printed in Great Britain by St. Edmundsbury Press, Bury St. Edmunds, Suffolk.

INDIAN RESTAURANT MENU

Appetisers

Dhokla 46
BAKED SEMOLINA SAVOURY SPONGE
*Home-style squares of warm savoury 'sponge' enhanced
with spicy piquant oil and garnished with fresh
coriander and coconut.*

Pakoras 48
VEGETABLE FRITTERS
*Lightly spiced mixed vegetable fritters in a crisp
and flavourful besan flour batter.*

Samosas 50
FILLED AND FRIED PASTRY TRIANGLES
*Crisply-fried filo pastry triangles filled with
a delicious potato or minced meat stuffing
and eaten hot from the pan.*

Payaz Bhajias. 51
ONION BHAJIAS
*Crunchy onion snacks to be eaten in
between meals or at the start
of a lunch or supper.*

Dahi Wada 52
SPICY DUMPLINGS IN YOGHURT SAUCE
*Fried lentil dumplings spiced with ginger and garlic
and served cold in a fragrant
yoghurt sauce.*

Upma 54
SEMOLINA SAVOURY

A honey-gold fried crumble laced with peas, cashews, chillies and mustard seeds, served hot in little bowls and eaten with spoons.

～

Eggs

Anda Akuri 56
SAVOURY SCRAMBLED EGGS

Parsee-style eggs, scrambled with onion, chilli and coriander and served hot with toast or Indian bread.

～

Nargesi Kofta 57
SPICY SCOTCH EGGS

An Anglo-Indian version of Scotch eggs, made with spiced savoury minced beef and accompanied by rice and pickles.

～

Goa Baida Kari 59
EGG CURRY WITH COCONUT

A Goan speciality made from hard-boiled eggs in a hot and spicy coconut sauce and served with rice.

～

Abla Anda Kari 60

HARD-BOILED EGG CURRY

*A mild to medium hot Anglo-Indian curry
served with rice and chutney.*

Seafood

Parsi Machi 62

PARSEE FISH

*Fish lightly fried with ginger, onion, chilli
and garlic then served in a mellow, egg-thickened
sweet-sour sauce and garnished with lemon.*

Machi Pullau 64

KEDGEREE INDIAN-STYLE

*A familiar Basmati rice and fish dish, finely flavoured
with coconut and assorted Indian spices.*

Dahi Machi 66

FISH IN COCONUT SAUCE

*Cubes of tender fish poached in a medium hot curry
and coconut sauce.*

Jinga Kari 67
PRAWN CURRY

*A medium creamy curry which will delight
those who love prawns.*

~

Jinga Tikka Kababs 68
KING PRAWN TIKKA KEBABS

*Succulent marinated king prawns baked on skewers
in a tandoor oven.*

~

Chicken

Murgh Tandoori 70
TANDOORI CHICKEN

*Chicken joints coated and marinated in a deep orange
curry paste and cooked in a tandoor until dry and crisp.
They are served with shredded lettuce, tomatoes,
onion rings, lemon and bread.*

~

Makhani Murgh 72
BUTTER CHICKEN

*Regally opulent, this is made from freshly-cooked tandoori
chicken reheated in a tomato sauce enriched with butter
and double cream. It is served with bread and
a selection of pickles.*

~

Murgh Tikka Kababs 74
CHICKEN TIKKA KEBABS

Skewers of tandoori-marinated chicken breast, baked in a tandoor oven and served with salad, fresh lime and bread.

〜

Bengal Murgh Tali 75
FRIED CHICKEN WITH GINGER

A speciality from Bengal, this is made from fried chicken portions flavoured with preserved ginger, garlic and chillies. It is delicately sweet and served with a potato dish and other vegetables to taste.

〜

Murgh Pakora 76
SPICED FRIED CHICKEN IN BESAN FLOUR

Flour-coated chicken portions, golden-fried with selected herbs and spices. They are served with a potato dish or other vegetables to taste.

〜

Murgh Musallam 78
MARINATED WHOLE CHICKEN

A spectacular royal dish from the Mogul Empire in which yoghurt-marinated chicken is filled with rice, peas and hard-boiled egg and braised in a rich and subtly-spiced sauce with ground almonds and poppy seeds.

〜

Murgh Simla 81
CHICKEN SIMLA

From the days of the Raj, this is an Anglo-Indian curry which is mild and laden with cream. It is accompanied with rice and mango chutney.

〜

Murgh Nizam 82
CHICKEN NIZAM

*Created in celebration of the Nizam of Hyderabad, this is
a succulent medium hot curry with mixed chillies, poppy
seeds, saffron, coconut and yoghurt. It is served with rice
and a separate vegetable curry.*

～

Murgh Moghlai 84
MAJESTIC CHICKEN

*A northern version of Murgh Nizam with its own majesty
and sophistication, it is creamy-rich with milk and
yoghurt, finely spiced and laced with dark poppy seeds,
flaked almonds and saffron. It is served with bread.*

～

Murgh Tikka Masala 86
CHICKEN TIKKA MASALA

*A mild and gentle yoghurt sauce, lightly coloured,
highlights one of India's most renowned chicken curries.
It is served with rice and separate vegetable dishes to
taste.*

～

Murgh Korma 88
CHICKEN KORMA

*Mild and refined, this is made from chicken breasts
simmered in a creamy sauce with a distinctive balance of
spices, ground almonds and cardamom. It is sprinkled with
toasted almond flakes and served with bread.*

～

Palek Murgh 90
CHICKEN AND SPINACH

*A mild and dryish curry with spinach, served with rice or
bread and a selection of raitas and chutney.*

～

Murgh Passanda 90
CHICKEN PASSANDA

A classic chicken dish from Hyderabad, this is a
beautifully seasoned and delicate curry served with rice.

⌐

Murgh Kari 91
CHICKEN CURRY

An Anglo-Indian curry with a wealth of exotic flavours,
this is served with rice, mango chutney and a selection
of raitas.

⌐

Murgh Jalfrezi 92
CHICKEN JALFREZI

Said to be a British invention, this Anglo-Indian curry is
dry and characterised by the inclusion of tomatoes and red
and green peppers. It is fairly hot and served with yoghurt
or raitas, mango chutney and bread.

⌐

Murgh Do-piaza 94
CHICKEN DO-PIAZA

A medium-hot chicken breast curry enlivened with onions
and thickened with yoghurt. Garnished with crisply fried
onions, it is served with rice and raitas.

⌐

Murgh Dhansak 96
CHICKEN DHANSAK

Originally from Persia, this is a hottish, marigold yellow
curry braised with lentils and tomatoes. It is served with
bread, raitas and chutney.

⌐

Murgh Madras 98
CHICKEN MADRAS

*A characterful hot curry served with raitas, chutney,
tomatoes, cucumber and plain boiled rice.*

Murgh Vindaloo 99
CHICKEN VINDALOO

*A fiery chicken and potato curry from Goa, not for the
faint-hearted, this is sharpened with vinegar and served
with rice, raitas, assorted pickles or chutney.*

Murgh Xacuti 100
CHICKEN XACUTI

*Stingingly hot, this is a deep brown and potent curry from
Goa. It is served with rice, lentil dhal and yoghurt
(if you dare).*

Meat

Bhoona Gosht 104
DRY LAMB CURRY

*A dryish fried curry, speckled with coconut and medium
hot, this is served with vegetables in sauce, raitas, chutney
and bread.*

Keema Matar 114
MINCED LAMB CURRY WITH PEAS

A subtle and medium hot minced lamb curry, coloured with peas, this is served with bread and pickles.

⌁

Gosht Rogan Josh 116
LAMB AND TOMATO CURRY

A vibrant, medium hot Kashmiri stew of simmered lamb and tomatoes thickened with ground almonds and yoghurt. It is served with bread.

⌁

Bhindi Gosht 118
LAMB AND OKRA STEW

A lamb, okra and yoghurt curry, mildly hot and eaten with bread.

⌁

Gosht Tikka Kababs 119
MEAT TIKKA KEBABS

Skewers of delicious tandooried lamb, served with lime, salad and bread.

⌁

Gosht Dhansak 119
LAMB DHANSAK

A variation on Murgh Dhansak, this time using lamb.

⌁

Gosht Do-piaza 119
LAMB DO-PIAZA

A finely-spiced lamb stew packed with onions and thickened with yoghurt. It is served with rice and raitas.

⌁

Gosht Korma 120
LAMB KORMA
A delicate dish, wonderfully creamy.

～

Gosht Kari 120
LAMB CURRY
A creamy, medium hot curry.

～

Phal Gosht 121
PORK PHAL
The hottest curry there is – be very careful.

～

Gosht Vindaloo 122
PORK VINDALOO
A breathtakingly hot curry from Goa made from pork and potatoes with a traditional splash of malt vinegar. It is served with plenty of rice, pickles and yoghurt.

～

Sorpotel 124
MEAT AND LIVER STEW
Another fiery combination from Goa and a relative of the vindaloo, serve this with rice and dhal to cool the palate.

～

Vegetables

Channa Masala 126
SAVOURY CHICK PEAS

A hearty and spicy dish, ideal as a main course for vegetarians or to accompany a meat dish. Serve with warm bread or rolls.

⁓

Rajma Masala 127
SAVOURY RED KIDNEY BEANS

Spiced and flavoursome kidney beans to make a tasty vegetarian meal.

⁓

Sabzi Ka Kari 128
VEGETABLE CURRY

A characterful, medium hot curry served with rice, chutney and other side dishes to taste.

⁓

Bhari Simla Mirich 130
STUFFED MIXED PEPPERS

Vegetable-filled peppers, simmered in a vibrant spicy tomato sauce. They can be eaten with rice or bread.

⁓

Aviyal 132
MIXED VEGETABLES IN CURRY SAUCE

A piquantly flavoured vegetable curry from Kerala in the south, lightened with coconut milk and served with rice and pickles or chutney.

Masala Bhindi 134
CURRIED OKRA

*A medium hot curry featuring exotically flavoured okra and
served with bread.*

~

Aloo Bombay 135
BOMBAY POTATOES

*Dry-fried spicy chunks of potato served as a side dish or
as part of a vegetarian meal.*

~

Aloo Methi 136
FRIED POTATOES WITH FENUGREEK

*To complement any meal, a dryish sauce coats the potatoes
flavoured with mild fenugreek leaves.*

~

Aloo Sag 137
POTATOES WITH SPINACH

*A full-strength potato and spinach combination, braised in
water with herbs and spices, this makes an appetising
side dish.*

~

Aloo Gobi 138
POTATOES WITH CAULIFLOWER

*Hot with spices and herbs coating the mouth-watering
combination of cauliflower and potatoes.*

~

Vegetarian Main Courses

Idlis 140
RICE CAKES

Small, snow-white and round spongy cakes made from urad dhal and individually steamed for perfect results. Serve with coconut chutney and raitas.

✎

Dosa 142
PANCAKES

Extra large and vegetable-filled fried pancakes which can be rolled, folded or twirled. They are one of the highlights of many an Indian vegetarian restaurant and magnificent with coconut chutney and Tarka Dhal.

✎

Sambhar 144
CURRIED LENTILS WITH VEGETABLES

An exceptionally tasty main course made from Tarka Dhal and assorted vegetables. The dish is garnished with crisply fried onions and served with rice.

✎

Matar Paneer 146
INDIAN CHEESE WITH MINT AND TOMATOES

A vegetarian curry of paneer with tomatoes and smooth yoghurt. It is served with bread and raitas.

✎

Palak Paneer Sak 148
INDIAN CHEESE WITH SPINACH AND CREAM

An appetising combination, richly endowed with a traditional Indian variety of herbs, spices and cream. It is served with bread.

⁓

Paneer 150
INDIAN CHEESE

A concentrated and firm white cows' milk cheese resembling tofu in appearance which features in many Indian vegetarian dishes.

⁓

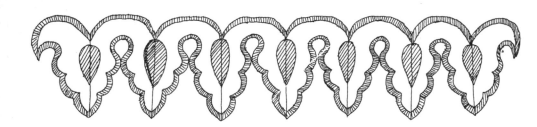

— Biriyanis —

Highly-prized and much respected combinations of exotically marinated chicken, meat, fish or vegetables, layered with saffron rice. The garnish is composed of fried onions, almonds, sliced hard-boiled eggs and raisins and any biriyani is a meal in itself. Chutney is an appropriate accompaniment.

Murgh Biriyani 152
CHICKEN BIRIYANI

Gosht Biriyani 154
BIRIYANI WITH LAMB

Jinga Biriyani 154
BIRIYANI WITH PRAWNS

Khumb Biriyani 154
BIRIYANI WITH MUSHROOMS

Accompaniments

Chawal 156
RICE
*Simply but perfectly boiled white basmati, ideal as an
accompaniment to many of the curries on the menu.*

❧

Chawal Pilau 156
SAVOURY RICE
A highly spiced, aromatic rice.

❧

Chawal Saffran 157
SAFFRON RICE
*A delicious rice with the delicate colour of saffron and
subtle flavour of spices.*

❧

Red and Yellow Rice 157

A colourful side-dish to complement any meal.

❧

Tarka Dhal 158
SPICY LENTILS
*A characterful and mildly curried pulse dish which can be
eaten as a main course with rice, or eaten with other
curry dishes.*

❧

Kari Dahl 159
CURRIED DAHL
A hotter version of Tarka Dhal.

~

Kitcherie 160
RICE AND GREEN LENTILS
A mild and substantial accompaniment to strong curries.

~

Tamattar Bhurta 161
TOMATO CHUTNEY
A cooling and exquisitely fragrant relish, recommended as the perfect accompaniment to hot curries.

~

Raitas
YOGHURT SIDE DISHES
Raitas are cooling yoghurt-based side dishes enhanced with fresh ingredients such as potatoes, carrot, mint, cucumber, coriander, banana and aubergines. They are well-spiced and mild to medium hot and team well with all curries.

~

Aloo Raita 162
POTATO RAITA

~

Gajar Raita 163
CARROT RAITA

~

Podeena Raita 163
MINT RAITA

~

Kheera Raita 164
CUCUMBER RAITA

~

Keela Raita 164
BANANA RAITA

Brinjal Raita 165
AUBERGINE RAITA

⁓

Pudina Chutney. 166
MINT CHUTNEY

*Mild-tasting and cool to the palate, this chutney goes well
with vegetarian dishes as well as the lamb-based Shami
Kababs and Shahi Kababs.*

⁓

Dahnia Chutney. 167
CORIANDER CHUTNEY

*A bright green condiment perfect to serve with almost any
Indian curry.*

⁓

Nariyal Chutney. 167
COCONUT CHUTNEY

*A flavourful blend of coconut and chopped coriander with
the addition of green chillies. Excellent with
vegetarian dishes.*

— Desserts —

Gulab Jamun 170

MILK DUMPLINGS IN SYRUP

The best known of Indian desserts, these warm fried
dumplings are made from a rich milk powder and soaked
in a voluptuous rose-scented syrup.

⌒

Mango Kulfi 172

MANGO ICE CREAM

One of India's greatest desserts, this wonderfully cooling
ice cream is spiked with cardamom and decorated
with chopped pistachio nuts.

⌒

Seviyan Kheer 173

VERMICELLI MILK PUDDING

A luxurious milk pudding with a hint of rose water made
from butter-fried vermicelli, flaked almonds and rich milk
and decorated with chopped pistachios.

⌒

Kheer 174

RICE PUDDING

A simple but captivating rice sweet with flaked almonds,
gently spiced with cardamom and perfumed with
rose water.

⌒

Firni 175
RICE CREAM

A lightly sweetened and intensely white ground rice pudding, resembling thin blancmange and flavoured with rose. It tastes delicious cold in small dishes and is cleansing and refreshing after a hot meal.

⌐

Shrikhand 176
YOGHURT AND SAFFRON DESSERT

Egg-yellow and deceptively rich-tasting, this simple yet exclusive dessert is served in small individual dishes and sometimes forms part of a vegetarian thali.

⌐

Tamattar Barfi 177
TOMATO FUDGE

Unique in the West, this sugary dessert which resembles fudge or candy is perfect to enjoy with strong tea or coffee at the end of a meal.

⌐

Panchamritam 178
FRUITED BANANA DESSERT

A southern Indian dessert, this dark brown, extraordinarily sweet confection is unusual and well worth sampling.

⌐

Gajar Ka Halwa 179
CARROT PUDDING

A top-class dessert and a popular choice, this is made from grated carrots simmered slowly in milk with sugar and spices until thick. It is utterly mouth-watering.

⌐

Drinks

Masala Chai 182
SPICED TEA
*Rich, milky, sweet and fragrant.
An unexpected pleasure.*

Lassi 183
YOGHURT DRINK
*The national drink of India,
a light and tangy yoghurt froth*

CONTENTS

INTRODUCTION

*S*een through Western eyes, India is a glitteringly bright sub-continent on a massive scale, a profusion of incessant noise and chatter, mystical, historic, vivacious, tinted like stained glass with brilliant green herbs and amber spices, blessed with luscious fruits and dazzling vegetables, religious, dusty, constantly bustling, part sultry and debilitatingly hot, part cool, pastoral and verdant; awesomely beautiful. It teems with monsoon rains and people, some poverty-stricken, others wealthy and cultivated, still more steering a middle course. It is made up of nine union territories and twenty-four states and within those states are countless castes which change every ten to fifteen miles, providing contrasts in lifestyle, eating patterns and culture. The main languages are Hindi and English but there are fourteen others besides and eight or more different religious groups actively practising their beliefs.

The Muslims, mostly in the north of India and also in pockets in other parts of the country, are keen meat eaters but pork is banned on religious grounds as it is considered a dirty animal with unsavoury habits. Fish and poultry are as much in favour as meat and all Muslim food is seasoned exquisitely and discreetly, often engulfed in yoghurt-rich sauces and subtly garnished. The Hindus, who make up the bulk of the population, are strict and vigilant vegetarians, believing the cow to be sacred and only recently eating unfertilised eggs. The Jewish orthodox community remain close to their kosher roots but understandably cook with an oriental bias. The remaining Portuguese Catholics in Goa, home of the vindaloo, are devoted pork eaters, as are other neighbouring Christians. The Parsees, Jains, Brahmans in the extreme north and the Syrian Catholics along the southwest coast all have their own culinary specialities and a few of these, with short explanations, have been included where appropriate.

Indian cooking, arguably the most exotic and colourful in the world, is almost a total free-for-all, Indian cooks individual to the nth degree and the interpretation of a particular dish rarely the same twice. But when you think about it and take into account whimsy on the part of the cook, mood also and the geography and climate of the country, how else can it be? There are no set culinary rules to follow as there are in the West. The combinations of ingredients vary from family to family and state to state and recipes as we understand them are not often written down but passed on verbally through the generations from grandmother to mother, mother to daughter, memsahib to servant. For the most part, theory plays only a miniscule role in the kitchen but practical skill is vital and this is learned by watching, absorbing and then doing, with a personal flourish here and there depending on how inventive and creative the cook wants to be. Ask any Asian lady in a bus queue, serving in a shop, nursing at the hospital how she makes, say, Gulab Jamun, and she tells you it's half a bowl of milk powder and some flour and some spices and some baking powder and oh yes, just enough water to make it soft, you know, a bit like your English pastry. Well, you sort of know. Fortunately, Indian friends rally round and come to the rescue with family recipes, books of old, scribbles in Hindi and samples. You learn the fundamentals easily enough.

Generally speaking, the ingredients used in the book can be found in leading supermarket chains in big cities and towns where there are ethnic communities. When something special has been used, be it a fresh or packeted product available only from an Indian outlet, I have said so in the introduction to the recipe.

A Short Anglo-Indian History

he following little piece was written by me well over twenty-five years ago when I was working on a project with the Indian High Commission. I found it amid some old papers on India and Indian food and it seems an apt way of summing up the enduring culinary relationship between Britain and India.

India in the seventeenth century had unique and enviable riches and dream-like splendours. The whole country gleamed and shone and overflowed with shimmering silver and gold brocades, fine calicos and muslins, beautifully woven silks and rare spices. It attracted traders from all over the world and as early as 1600, Queen Elizabeth I granted a royal charter to the East India Company whose merchant members set up trading posts throughout India, especially to purchase the fabulous luxuries that were in such demand. The British merchants mingled freely and happily with their Indian colleagues and in time they not only adopted the habits and customs of the country, but many married the more cultivated women of high castes, forging strong Anglo-Indian ties.

When these men returned to Britain with their wives, families and Asian servants, the oriental way of life came with them. Their cuisine was mostly Indian. Friends were introduced for the first time to highly spiced curry dishes and unusual condiments. Recipes passed from hand to hand and slowly, over the years, interest in Indian food grew to such an extent that whole chapters on the preparation of curry powders and curry dishes were to be found in cookery books of the period.

Later on in 1858, Queen Victoria's government took control of the East India Company and British civil servants and army officials, accompanied by their wives and families, went to India to replace the merchant traders. This strata of society – perhaps more conservative in taste and outlook than the merchants before them – found it difficult at first to adapt to an entirely new and sometimes strange environment and it was some time before the majority accepted the Eastern tempo and learned to regard the traditions, fashions and eating habits of India with pleasure instead of suspicion.

On their return to Britain, many retired service officials tried to recapture something of the oriental pattern that had become so much part of their lives and it was they who were largely responsible for creating a new wave of interest in Indian food. Curry eating once again became fashionable and in the winter of 1926, the first Indian restaurant in Europe was opened in London's Gerrard Street, Soho, by a Mr Shaffi. This was followed shortly afterwards by Veeraswamy's and since then the growth of Indian restaurants has become so prolific that there is barely a large city in Britain without one. It is not only the novelty of the food that attracts. Quality and quantity, coupled with polite and conscientious service and peaceful surroundings, make eating in Indian restaurants an unrivalled and satisfying pleasure.

THE INDIAN KITCHEN – BASIC EQUIPMENT FOR SUCCESS

KARAHI

Almost identical to a Chinese wok, the karahi is a pan with one looped handle on each side and is made in assorted sizes of heavy metal to withstand high heat and sometimes naked flames. The karahi has become synonymous with Balti cooking (see page 44).

TAVA

Made from heavy metal, flat and almost the same as a Western griddle, this is used for cooking Indian flat breads such as chapati and paratha.

TANDOOR OVEN

An unglazed clay oven, fired with charcoal, this looks a bit like an open-topped beehive and there is a gap in the base to ensure the flow of air is working efficiently. Flattened and dampened naan and roti breads are put on to something which I can best describe as an outsize mushroom lined with a floured cloth and then slapped internally against the sides of the oven until cooked through and well browned. It takes skill and practice to do this properly and I appreciate all the lessons given to me by the cooks at the Karahi King restaurant in North Wembley. Other techniques for transferring the bread to the hot oven do exist. A tandoor oven is also used for cooking meat and chicken. See Murgh Tandoori (page 70).

THALI

This is a circular tray, usually of stainless steel or brass, on which individual bowls of food are placed. Each person has his own thali and all the dishes for the meal are served together, sweet and savoury. As the tray is capacious, breads are added to complete the meal. A typical thali, the kind served at the Diwana restaurant, in London's Euston, would comprise rice, dhal, vegetable curries and chapatis or pooris. Likewise, a luxury one would have dhal, rice, a selection of curries, pickles, condiments and the same breads. The dessert is usually Shrikhand (see page 176). A thali meal is most usually served in a vegetarian restaurant.

GLOSSARY OF INGREDIENTS

A guide to some of the ingredients used in the book.

Asafoetida (Hing)
Gum resin from Afghanistan and Iranian plants with a strong and pungent smell, asafoetida is reminiscent of garlic in concentrated form. It is used in tiny amounts in Indian cooking to reduce flatulence and is considered an anti-spasmodic.

Bay Leaves (Teipattar)
Leaves from an evergreen plant with an unmistakable and aromatic scent, they are generally used dry and much liked in the north.

Breads
Indian breads need skill and expertise for success and now that so many are nationally available from supermarkets and Indian shops, there seems no point in providing you with time-consuming and complex recipes. Buying is the best answer. Poppadums can also be found everywhere, both cooked and uncooked.

For clarity, descriptions of the different breads are:

Bhatura: Deep fried discs of bread, made from white dough raised with yoghurt and bicarbonate of soda.

Chapati: Almost pancake-like, chapati is flat bread made from a type of wholemeal flour called atta. It is dry-fried on both sides on a flat griddle (tava) and eaten with all meals throughout the day. It is India's national bread.

Naan: A yeasted and chewy flattish bread made from white flour, usually in a round or oblong shape, naan is cooked in a tandoor and can be plain or flavoured with herbs. When served in some Balti houses (page 44), it is so large that it has to be supported by at least two waiters!

Paratha: Puffy wholemeal bread, this starts out flat, is carefully and repeatedly rolled and folded to make it flaky. I have seen each portion skilfully wound round an index finger, removed, rolled out, placed on a ghee-brushed tava, brushed with more ghee and fried on both sides until golden brown. It is one of the richest of all Indian breads and tastes delicious.

Paratha, Stuffed: A speciality of the north, these are a kind of warm sandwich with a filling of spicy potatoes or sometimes meat.

Puri: A small ball of wholemeal dough (the same as chapati), this is rolled into a disc and deep-fried. It puffs up like a ball with a hollow centre. Sometimes the middle of the hollow is broken and the puri filled with a vegetable or chick pea curry.

Roti: A variation of chapati.

Cardamom (Illaichi)

Related to ginger and available in Britain in black and green pods, the milder seeds of the green are generally used in cooking and often ground up before use in a coffee grinder or with a pestle and mortar. It is a beautifully fragrant spice and the mainstay of Indian spice combinations.

Chilli, Green (Sabz Mirch)

Choose from small, medium or large fresh varieties which are carrot-shaped but more slender. The larger the pepper the milder the flavour. Seeds should be removed and discarded to reduce heat. Don't confuse these with large green peppers (bell peppers).

A piece of wisdom I came across in an old leaflet on spices: you can always make a curry hotter by adding chilli but you can never cool it down once it has cooked. Therefore add chilli and other hot spices judiciously unless you want fire food.

Chilli, Red (Lal Mirch)

This is hot, and is used as whole dried pods or ground. To subdue the heat, remove and discard seeds from whole pods, scrubbing your hands carefully afterwards to prevent burns to eyes and mouth should you touch these parts of the face by accident. Cayenne pepper equals chilli powder but chilli seasoning is no substitute as it is essentially a blend of spices for Mexican food, dark red and fairly mild.

Cinnamon (Dalchini)

Native to the Far East and produced from the dried bark of an evergreen tree belonging to the laurel family, cinnamon is available in stick form or ground. It is sweet-smelling and pleasingly fragrant.

Clove (Laung)

The unopened and dried bud of an evergreen tree native to South-east Asia, I once described clove in another book as having a spiky and pungent flavour and there's no mistaking it.

Coconut Milk

You can use canned coconut milk which is creamy-thick and luxurious, instant coconut powder which blends easily with warm water, or pieces of coconut cream, cut from a block, which also mixes to a creamy consistency in hot liquids and may be added directly to a curry mixture and stirred in gently until melted. You can make your own coconut milk by mixing 75 ml/5 tbsp desiccated coconut with enough hot water to cover, leaving it to brew for 30 minutes, whizzing until smooth in a blender and then straining.

Coriander, Fresh (Hara Dhaniya)

Also known as dizzycorn, Chinese parsley and cilantro, coriander is the most versatile fresh herb of all and its deep green leaves and stems add the characteristic Indian flavour when used in cooking or as a garnish. It is sold in packets in supermarkets, is readily available in bundles from fruit and vegetable markets and is always to be found in ethnic food shops – Greek, Chinese, Middle Eastern and of course Indian.

Coriander (Dhaniya)

Totally different in flavour from its fresh green counterpart, coriander is available in seed form which varies in colour from cream to light brown. Related to the parsley family, the seeds are reminiscent of sage and lemon mixed together. They are used whole or ground in cooking and are one of the ingredients of curry powder.

Cumin (Jeera)

Native to India, the taste of cumin is distinctive and exquisitely fragrant and the spice is much used in cooking and also added to curry powder. It comprises the small dried fruit of an ornamental plant related to parsley.

Curry Leaves (Karipatta)

Available fresh or dried from Indian shops, the leaves grow on trees native to Asia and are small and bright green when fresh. As they dry, the colour darkens. They are used in vegetarian dishes and popular in southern India.

Curry Powder

Curry powder is not used by Indian cooks to any extent as they prefer to make up their own blends immediately prior to cooking from carefully selected spices.

Fennel Seeds (Sauf)

Another member of the parsley family, fennel seeds taste faintly of aniseed and are considered a digestive. The colour varies from yellowy-brown to green and they are much used in the north of the country.

Fenugreek (Methi)

Related to the pea family, the seeds of the plant are oval, darkish yellow and short with a kickback of caramel or burnt sugar. The spice is always used in small quantities because it can taste slightly bitter. It is recommended for vegetables such as aubergine (egg plant) and potatoes.

Fenugreek Leaves (Methi)

Available from Indian shops tied in bundles, the leaves are small and green and compatible with vegetable dishes and salads.

Garam Masala

Garam masala is the equivalent of mixed spice in the West and is a blend of non-hot spices which are used to flavour every kind of dish you can think of from curries to the occasional pudding. All the ready-prepared blends on the market are of a high standard but should you choose to make your own in line with Indian cooks, the following combination is a well-balanced mix. Keep it tightly stoppered in a jar or plastic container and, for freshness, store in the refrigerator if space permits. Given time, inclination and a solid blender or food processor, make a fresh batch of the masala (in smallish quantities) for every four to five dishes you plan on cooking.

45 ml/3 tbsp coriander seeds
Seeds from 2 black cardamom pods
15 ml/1 tbsp ground mace

10 ml/2 tsp cumin seeds
5 ml/1 tsp cloves
10 ml/2 tsp fennel seeds
2 bay leaves
5 cm/2 in piece cinnamon stick

1. Put all the spices listed above in a small saucepan.

2. Stand pan over a low heat and dry-fry for seconds rather than minutes. When ready, there will be a waft of aromatic fragrance.

3. Remove the pan from the heat straight away, cool the spices down until almost cold then work to a powder in a food processor or mortar and pestle.

Garlic (Lasan)

Potent raw but less so when cooked, garlic must be the most widely used herb in the world and was popular in England in the sixteenth century, during the reign of Queen Elizabeth I. It is a close relative of the onion but grows in bulbs containing clusters of individual sections or cloves, each individually wrapped in a papery skin which has to be removed before cooking.

Ghee

Most of the fat used by Indians in cooking is what is commonly called ghee and is nothing more complex than clarified butter. It is sold in cans in Britain and is excellent for frying as it can be heated to a high temperature without burning. Concentrated butter, available from some large supermarket chains, is one and the same and is also competitively priced. Vegetable ghee, now more widely used by the Indian community for health reasons, can be found in blocks in packets and is made from vegetable oil (which solidifies) together with natural colour such as beta-carotene and flavourings. It looks and tastes exactly like clarified butter.

Ginger (Adrak)

The rhizome of a perennial and tuberous plant, something like the lily. When fresh, the shape is literally all over the place and knobbly; the skin is beige while the inside flesh is fibrous. It adds an elusive subtlety to Indian cooking: slightly peppery, warm, pungent, penetrating. Ground ginger is made from year-old, sun-dried plants.

Herb Combinations

Every country has a group of flavours that give the food its own native and characteristic taste and in India it's fresh garlic, fresh ginger, onion and green chillies chopped together or ground to a paste in a blender or food processor. It's these four, primarily, which Indianise a dish.

Kewra (Screwpine)

A less refined substitute for rose water, this is available from Indian shops.

Mace (Javatri)

The mesh-like outer covering of nutmeg, the colour of mace is deepish orange and the taste is akin to nutmeg, though more subtle and exotic. It is economically priced in Indian shops but very costly everywhere else.

Mint (Podina)

A worldwide favourite, mint is highly prized in Indian cuisine and is a perennial plant native to western Asia and the Mediterranean. There are many varieties but all have a strong and pungent taste. Rarely in India is mint used for garnishing.

Mustard (Sarson/Rai)

Mustard seeds can be black or creamy-yellow and come from an annual plant related to the cabbage family. They are perfectly rounded and tend to leap up and down in the pan during preliminary frying, hence the need for a lid. They are surprisingly mild but have a definite flavour and are well suited to most curry dishes.

Nigella (Aiwain)

Small and darkish brown oval seeds with a mild, almost smoky aroma, they have a slight pepperiness about them and are used as a flavouring in pickles and also dishes from the eastern regions.

Nutmeg (Jaiphal)

The walnut-like seed of a plant resembling the peach which grows on tall, evergreen trees, nutmeg is used sparingly in Indian cooking due to its strength and potency. Mace is preferred.

Oils (Ka Tail or Tel)

Throughout the book, I have used sunflower or corn oil for most of the recipes but alternative oils, ghee or concentrated butter may be substituted if preferred. In India, different oils are used according to region, as follows:

Groundnut (Moongphali): Much appreciated in the south where peanuts grow profusely, this is also used in the western province of Maharashtra.

Sesame (Gingilly): The darker the colour, the deeper the flavour – nutty and characteristically exotic, sesame oil is favoured in the extreme south (Tamil Nadu) and also Maharashtra. India is a major exporter of the oil which is used in the West for the production of margarine.

Mustard (Sarson/Rai): Deep yellow and with a pronounced flavour, this oil is used primarily in the north and the eastern region of Bengal. It is highly recommended for fish frying.

Coconut (Copra): Mild and delicate and used in the extreme south-west, in the Kerala region, coconut oil solidifies in the cold.

Paprika (Deghi Mirch)
A bright orange-red powder, originally from Central America, but also grown in the area of Kashmir. It is mildly hot and made from sweet red peppers (capsicums).

Poppy Seeds (Khuskhus)
From scarlet poppies, these can be cream or grey-black. They are round, tiny, very mild and often used with other ingredients to add the merest hint of discretion to a curry dish. Poppy seeds are also useful as a thickening agent. They have no narcotic properties whatsoever.

Rose Water
This is used extensively in dessert dishes such as Gulab Jamun and sometimes Kulfi (ice cream) and can usually be ordered in advance from pharmacies. It can also be found in Indian shops, mostly in well sealed plastic bottles. Concentrated culinary rose essence can be used instead, but with great care as it is strong and potent.

Saffron (Zaffron/Kesar)
Tinting food golden yellow and with the most distinguished and unique taste of any spice, saffron comes from the dried stamens of a specially

cultivated crocus and is grown mostly in the north of India, in and around Kashmir. It is said to be the most expensive spice in the world, is deep orange in colour and available in strands or ground. In order to release its remarkable colour and perfume, the strands need a few minutes soaking in hot water or milk before use in cooking.

Sauces and Gravies

Not much liquid is added to Indian recipes and the ingredients are allowed to simmer gently in their own juices. If you prefer thinner sauces, add a little boiling water or stock at the end of cooking. Authentic dishes are rarely thickened with flour or cornflour but rather with poppy seeds, coconut itself or milk, ground nuts like almonds, and yoghurt.

Spices

To save confusion, it is always advisable to give the Indian name when buying spices in an Indian shop as sometimes the staff are unfamiliar with its Western equivalent.

Turmeric (Haldi)

Used in the West for piccalilli and mustard pickles, mild and gentle turmeric is responsible for adding a golden glow to Indian food. Of itself, it is a bright yellow powder and comes from an aromatic rhizome of the ginger family.

Yoghurt

Use natural yoghurt in the recipes, thick-set where indicated. For a milder, cooler aftertaste, you can use fromage frais in place of yoghurt.

EATING INDIAN-STYLE

*I*ndian families gather round the eating area in groups and all the food for the meal is put before them; there is no such thing as courses for appetisers, main courses and desserts as we understand them in the West. In fact, one of the desserts in the book called Firni, a light and delicate rice cream, is sometimes eaten at the beginning of the meal before the savouries.

Although perhaps a generalisation, Indian food becomes hot, hotter, hottest as one moves from north to south, changing from its mellow, creamy and temperate character in the cooler north to stingingly hot fire-brand curries in the steamy heat of the south and west – just think of Goa and its throat-grabbing vindaloo.

If you are in a typically Indian restaurant where members of the community congregate, you will notice that some people eat with the fingers of their right hand, often scooping up the food with bread. This is partly for reasons of hygiene as well-washed hands are considered cleaner than cutlery.

BALTI COOKING AND BALTI HOUSES

*I*t started in Birmingham back in the 1960s, has crept to Stoke-on-Trent and we were told about it by an old Brummie college friend and her husband when they were with us on a recent visit. To their astonishment, we'd never heard of Balti anything. 'What,' cried Jean, you've not had Balti cooking? Oh good gracious, come to us and we'll take you to our favourite Balti House in Sparkbrook, known at home as the Balti Belt.' So we did just that, on the spur of the moment, catching the fastest Intercity we could muster from Watford Junction. We spent a long evening feasting like Rajahs on a slap-up North-West Frontier meal at ridiculously low cost by any standards anywhere and came away converted to a masterful and genuine cuisine cooked by artists.

Balti cooking is, basically, wok cooking Indian-style, characterfully Muslim, no frills or fancies, bring your own booze and/or have a jug (huge) of ice cold Lassi, the biggest bargain of all time at pennies a glass instead of the pounds it costs in London and the South-East. The exquisitely spiced food, be it meat, poultry or vegetables, comes to you in a karahi, a two-handled black metal dish, too hot to touch, and alongside is freshly tandoored naan bread, so enormous that it has to be carried to the table by two waiters. You gape in wonder, break off bits and scoop up the food in the dish with your fingers in honest Indian style. Local patrons – professionals, yuppies, students, families and tourists – rarely, if ever, resort to cutlery because it's against Muslim religious beliefs and their attitude to hygiene. You soon learn.

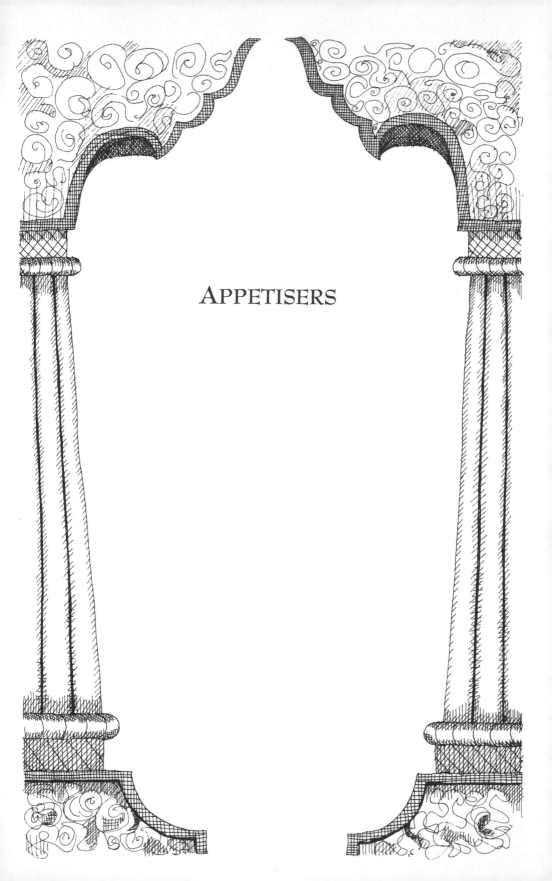

APPETISERS

DHOKLA

BAKED SEMOLINA SAVOURY SPONGE

ight, spongy, moist and quite one of the most delicious of all Indian savouries, dhokla from Gujarat is a superior and fine-flavoured snack food, often served cut up on its own with a hot drink and warmly welcomed by vegetarians. Although not often seen on menus, I have included it in the book because it has become a personal passion of mine. So much so, that I tried out fourteen different dhoklas before settling for this one which was given the seal of approval by the critical and gourmet husband of a dear Gujarati friend. Curiously, the raising agent used by most Indian cooks is Eno's (once called Eno's Fruit Salts), my late Mother's lifelong answer to indigestion and available from pharmacies nationwide.

Serves about 8

175 g	semolina (cream of wheat)	6 oz/1 cup
25 g	besan or gram flour	1 oz/¼ cup
25 g	rice flour	1 oz/¼ cup
5 ml	salt	1 tsp
1.25 ml	turmeric	¼ tsp
5 ml	ground cumin	1 tsp
2.5 ml	chilli powder	½ tsp
1 cm	piece fresh ginger, peeled and finely chopped	½ in
1	medium green chilli, deseeded	1
150 ml	yoghurt	¼ pt/⅔ cup
150 ml	warm water	¼ pt/⅔ cup
15 ml	oil, at room temperature	1 tbsp
10 ml	Eno's	2 tsp

FLAVOURED OIL (TARKA):

15 ml	oil	1 tbsp
5 ml	black mustard seeds	1 tsp
2.5 ml	chilli powder or paprika for mildness	½ tsp

GARNISH :
Chopped fresh coriander (cilantro)
Desiccated (shredded) coconut (optional)

1. Place a shallowish metal rack on to the base of a fairly large saucepan and add cold water until it is just level with the top of the rack.

2. Cover a matching saucepan lid with a large tea towel, placing it underneath to begin with then bringing the ends over the top and tying them round the knob with thin string. The towel absorbs steam and prevents the Dhokla from drying out. Slowly bring the water in the pan to a gentle boil.

3. Well grease and base line a 20 cm/8 in sandwich tin (pan) with a round of non-stick baking paper.

4. Tip the semolina into a bowl. Sift in the gram flour with the rice flour, salt, turmeric, cumin and chilli powder.

5. Add the ginger and chilli with the yoghurt and water, then quickly mix in the oil and Eno's. At this stage, the mixture will foam slightly.

6. Spread into the prepared tin (pan) and carefully transfer to the rack in the saucepan. Cover with the towel-covered lid and cook, without looking, for 15 minutes.

7. Turn off the heat and prepare the tarka. Heat the oil in a pan, add the mustard seeds and two-thirds cover with a lid. Fry for about 40 seconds until all the spluttering has subsided. Stir in the chilli powder or paprika.

8. Remove the tin or pan of dhokla from the saucepan. Turn out on to a wire rack and peel away the lining paper. Invert with a second rack so that the top of the dhokla is uppermost.

9. Cover with the tarka, then sprinkle with the coriander and coconut if using. Slide on to a board and cut into smallish squares. Serve just warm.

Tip: Cover leftovers and reheat in the microwave.

PAKORAS

VEGETABLE FRITTERS

old on almost every Indian street corner and appetisingly crunchy and golden, pakoras have become part of our Western lives, amiable and acceptable as snack food or starters for young and old alike. They are uncomplicated to make and absolutely stunning when served fresh and piping hot. The Indian flour needed for the batter is available from some of the larger supermarket chains and is the delicate yellow colour of semolina (cream of wheat).
Makes 12–15

	BATTER:	
225 g	besan or gram flour	8 oz/2 cups
75 g	plain (all-purpose) flour	3 oz/¾ cup
2.5 ml	baking powder	½ tsp
5 ml	salt	1 tsp
2.5 ml	EACH ground ginger, coriander (cilantro), cumin and turmeric	½ tsp
2.5 ml	chilli powder (optional)	½ tsp
5 ml	garam masala	1 tsp
about 300 ml	cold water	½ pt/1¼ cups

VEGETABLE SELECTION:
½ small cauliflower
1 carrot
1 onion
1 small aubergine (eggplant)
1 potato, peeled and cooked
Oil for deep-frying

1. To make the batter, sift all the dry ingredients together into a bowl.

2. Gradually whisk in the water and continue to whisk until the batter is smooth and without lumps. It should look like thickish cream.

3. Prepare the vegetables. Shred the cauliflower florets, discarding the stalks. Peel and grate the carrot and onion. Wash and dry the aubergine, leave on the skin and grate. Finely dice the potato.

4. Stir all the vegetables into the batter then drop tablespoons of the mixture into hot and sizzling oil. Fry about 4–5 at a time, allowing 5–7 minutes, and turn over at least twice with a wooden spoon so that the pakoras cook and brown evenly.

5. Transfer to a plate lined with scrunched up kitchen paper and drain thoroughly. Eat straight away.

SAMOSAS

FILLED AND FRIED PASTRY TRIANGLES

ou can buy these anywhere and everywhere in India and Britain, but with frozen filo pastry to hand in packets, samosas are hassle-free to make and crackling with crunch when eaten fresh from the fryer and still hot. You can use either of the fillings or make half a quantity of each.

Makes 12

Potato Filling
(see Dosa, page 142), cooled

Meat Filling
(see Keema Matar, page 114), cold

6 sheets filo pastry
Oil for deep-frying

1. Defrost 6 sheets of filo pastry and cut each in half lengthwise.

2. Put 2–3 tbsp of either filling on to one end of the strip then dampen all the edges facing you with a brush dipped in water. Fold over to make a triangle, completely enclosing the filling, and continue to fold the strip over and over and from side to side until all the strip has been used up. At this stage you should have a well-wrapped triangle with the filling deeply tucked inside.

3. Deep-fry about 4 at a time, in hot oil until well browned. Allow about 4 minutes and turn over once or twice with a spoon.

4. Drain well on a plate lined with scrunched up kitchen paper and, if possible, eat straight away.

PAYAZ BHAJIAS

ONION BHAJIAS

ade properly, these onion snacks from northern India are one of the delights of the Indian kitchen and can be eaten in between meals or at the beginning of a lunch or supper. They are no harder to cook at home than the pakoras but for total ease you can buy packets of bhajia mix which do a good enough job.
Makes 12–16

Batter (see Pakoras, page 48)
3 onions, sliced into thin rings
Oil for frying

1. Make up a pakora batter as given in the recipe on page 48, increasing the salt to 10 ml/2 tsp and colouring the mixture pinky-orange with 1–2 drops of edible red food colouring.

2. Combine the onions with the batter mixture and don't be deterred by what appears to be too many onions to batter – they will hold together in flattish rounds when fried, rather like hamburgers in shape.

3. Fry tablespoons of the mixture in hot oil in a large, shallow frying pan. Flatten them out with the back of a spoon as they cook and fry for about 5 minutes or until golden brown and crisp, turning twice.

4. Drain well and serve as hot as you like.

DAHI WADA

SPICY DUMPLINGS IN YOGHURT SAUCE

A top-class vegetarian cold starter from the west and north, this is substantial enough to double as a main course. A visit to an Indian shop or large supermarket in a major town may be necessary to find the white pulse called urad dhal, which is the main ingredient of the dumplings. A food processor will be needed for success.
     Serves 6

225 g	white urad dhal	8 oz/1 cup
	Cold water	
	1 small onion, chopped	
	1 clove garlic, chopped	
1 cm	fresh ginger, peeled and chopped	½ in
	1 green chilli, deseeded and halved	
5 ml	cumin seeds	1 tsp
10 ml	coriander (cilantro) seeds	2 tsp
7.5 ml	salt	1½ tsp
45 ml	besan or gram flour	3 tbsp
1.25 ml	bicarbonate of soda (baking soda)	¼ tsp
	Oil for deep-frying	

YOGHURT SAUCE:		
450 ml	liquid, unset yoghurt	¾ pt/2 cups
7.5 ml	salt	1½ tsp
5 ml	ground cumin	1 tsp
2.5 ml	chilli powder	½ tsp
2.5 ml	freshly ground black pepper	½ tsp
150 ml	cold water	¼ pt/⅔ cup
30 ml	chopped fresh coriander (cilantro)	2 tbsp

1. To make the dumplings, soak the urad dhal in plenty of cold water for 6–8 hours at room temperature. Keep covered.

2. Drain and scrape into a food processor bowl. Add the onion, garlic, ginger, chilli, cumin seeds, coriander seeds and the remaining dry ingredients.

3. Process for 5 minutes, pulsing on and off and giving it short bursts in between to prevent the motor from overheating.

4. Scrape the mixture into a bowl. Cover and refrigerate for 1 hour.

5. Half-fill a deep pan with oil and heat until hot. Carefully drop in tablespoons of mixture, allowing 4 at a time to make 4 dumplings. Fry for about 4–5 minutes or until light golden brown. Turn over once with a spoon so that they cook evenly. Transfer to a large plate lined with scrunched up kitchen paper. Repeat, using up rest of mixture.

6. For the sauce, whisk all the ingredients until smooth. Pour into a fairly large, shallow dish and add the hot dumplings. Toss over in the sauce, chill and sprinkle with coriander before serving.

UPMA

SEMOLINA SAVOURY

lmost like a savoury crumble top, upma is usually eaten in the south as a hot snack between meals or for breakfast with milk and is a completely off-beat delicacy. It is traditional to cook the upma in a type of karahi but any strong and deep non-stick frying pan will do.
Serves 6–7

175 g	semolina (cream of wheat)	6 oz/1 cup
30 ml	oil	2 tbsp
5 ml	white mustard seeds	1 tsp
	2 green chillies, deseeded	
	1 onion, chopped	
30 ml	salted cashew nuts	2 tbsp
	Pinch of asafoetida	
750 ml	warm water	1¼ pts/3 cups
50 g	frozen peas, thawed	2 oz/½ cup
5 ml	salt	1 tsp
	Chopped fresh coriander (cilantro)	

1. Dry roast the semolina slowly in a heavy frying pan and stir almost continually with a wooden spoon until pale golden.

2. Heat the oil in a large non-stick frying pan. Add the mustard seeds and two-thirds cover with a lid. Cook until the seeds stop spluttering. Reduce the heat to low.

3. Add the chillies, onion, cashew nuts and asafoetida. Add the browned semolina, water, peas and salt. Cook, stirring all the time, until the mixture comes to the boil. Lower the heat and cover.

4. Simmer gently for 10 minutes, stirring often, when the mixture should be thick and the semolina well cooked. Serve in bowls, each portion sprinkled with coriander.

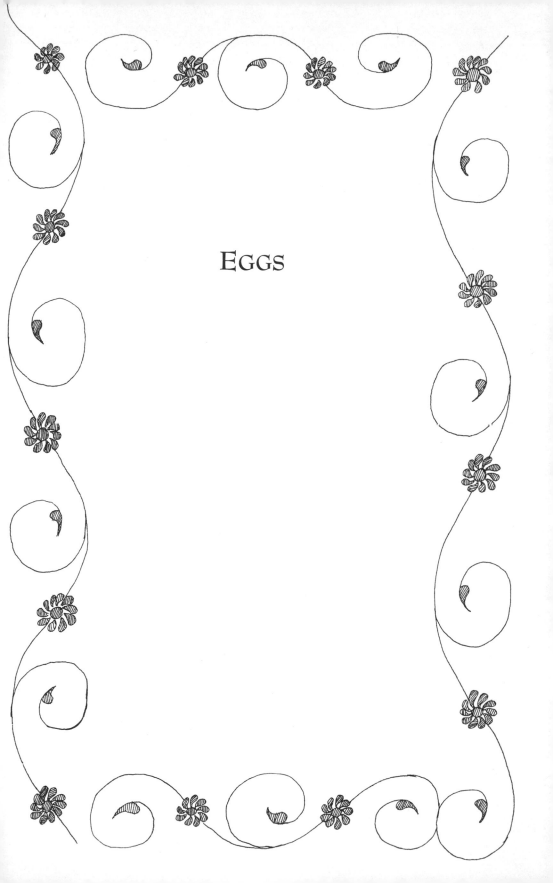

EGGS

ANDA AKURI

SAVOURY SCRAMBLED EGGS

he Parsees in the north have a knack with eggs and specialise in these spiced and scrambled ones which team up happily with brown toast or any Indian bread, toasted or not, but warm for preference.

Serves 4

	6 large eggs	
45 ml	milk	3 tbsp
	1 onion, chopped	
	1 green chilli, deseeded and finely chopped	
15 ml	oil	1 tbsp
30 ml chopped fresh coriander (cilantro)		2 tbsp
	3-4 large pinches of salt	

1. Beat the eggs and milk well together, cover and leave on one side for the moment.

2. Fry the onion and chilli gently in a saucepan with the oil until just beginning to turn a light gold.

3. Add the eggs, coriander and salt. Scramble lightly, stirring all the time, until the mixture just sets. Serve straight away with freshly made toast or bread.

NARGESI KOFTA

SPICY SCOTCH EGGS

A souvenir from the days of the Raj, these Indian-style coated and fried hard-boiled eggs closely resemble Scotch eggs and can be treated as a main course with chutney or pickle and rice, or be featured on any party buffet for a splash of colour. The Indian name Nargesi is said to mean narcissus, like the appearance of the eggs when halved.
Serves 6

	6 large eggs	
	MEAT MIXTURE:	
450 g	lean minced (ground) steak	1 lb
5 ml	salt	1 tsp
5 ml	garam masala	1 tsp
5 ml	medium curry powder	1 tsp
10 ml	ground cumin	2 tsp
5 ml	ground coriander (cilantro)	1 tsp
	1 clove garlic, crushed	
	2 large eggs, beaten	
30 ml	besan or gram flour	2 tbsp
	COATING:	
	1 large egg, beaten	
10 ml	water	2 tsp
120 ml	crisp breadcrumbs	8 tbsp
	Oil for deep-frying	

1. Hard boil and shell the eggs and leave on one side.

2. Combine all the meat mixture ingredients together well and knead with your hands until smooth. Divide into 6 equal portions.

3. Wrap evenly round the eggs and leave in the cool for 1 hour.

4. For coating, beat the egg and water well together in a bowl. Add the covered eggs, coat each one thoroughly then toss in the breadcrumbs. Leave for about 15 minutes in a cool place.

5. Deep-fry in hot oil for 10–12 minutes, turning over 2 or 3 times with a spoon.

6. Drain on a plate lined with crumpled kitchen paper. Halve lengthwise when cold.

GOA BAIDA KARI

EGG CURRY WITH COCONUT

 hottish egg main course from the west, this is best served with plain boiled rice.

Serves 4

	8 large eggs	
	1 large onion, sliced	
	1 clove garlic, sliced	
2.5 cm	piece fresh ginger, peeled and sliced	1 in
15 ml	oil	1 tbsp
5 ml	ground cumin	1 tsp
5 ml	ground coriander (cilantro)	1 tsp
5 ml	garam masala	1 tsp
2.5 ml	turmeric	½ tsp
1.25 ml	chilli powder	¼ tsp
60 ml	instant coconut powder	4 tbsp
150 ml	warm water	¼ pt/⅔ cup
5 ml	salt	1 tsp

1. Hard boil and shell the eggs. Leave aside.

2. Grind the onion, garlic and ginger to a coarse paste then fry in the oil in a saucepan until pale gold.

3. Add all the ground spices and fry for about 45 seconds then splash in a few drops of cold water to stop the mixture burning.

4. Blend the coconut powder smoothly with the water and stir into the fried ingredients with the salt.

5. Bring to the boil, stirring. Lower the heat and add the eggs one at a time with a tablespoon. Cover and heat through gently for 10 minutes.

ABLA ANDA KARI

HARD-BOILED EGG CURRY

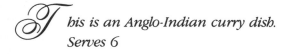 *his is an Anglo-Indian curry dish.*
Serves 6

12 eggs
Vegetable curry sauce (see Sabzi Ka Kari, page 128)
30 ml   desiccated (shredded) coconut   2 tbsp

1. Hard boil and shell the eggs. Leave aside.

2. Make the sauce as on page 128, stirring in the desiccated coconut.

3. Add the eggs to the sauce and heat through gently for about 5 minutes.

4. Serve with rice and mango chutney.

SEAFOOD

PARSI MACHI

PARSEE FISH

A medium-hot fish dish from the north, this is slightly sweet-sour and quite different from most standard Indian recipes I've come across. It is thickened, Western-style, with a beaten egg, cornflour and vinegar mix and is delicious with haddock, hake or salmon cutlets; not cod as it tends to be too flaky and might therefore disintegrate.
Serves 4

	4 medium-sized firm fish cutlets	
	1 large onion, chopped	
	2–3 cloves garlic, crushed	
	1 cm piece fresh ginger, peeled and chopped	½ in
	2 green chillies, deseeded	
15 ml	oil	1 tbsp
5 ml	ground cumin	1 tsp
5 ml	garam masala	1 tsp
300 ml	hot water	½ pt/1¼ cups

	TO THICKEN:	
15 ml	cornflour (cornstarch)	1 tbsp
60 ml	cold water	4 tbsp
30 ml	malt vinegar	2 tbsp
	1 large egg, beaten	
30 ml	mango chutney	2 tbsp
	4 lemon wedges	

1. Wash and dry the fish and leave aside in a cool place.

2. Grind the onion, garlic and ginger to a paste with the chillies.

3. Fry in the oil in a fairly large frying pan until light golden, keeping the heat fairly low. Add the cumin and garam masala, increase the heat and stir-fry for 20 seconds.

4. Pour in the water, bring to a gentle boil and stir well to combine. Cover and simmer for 10 minutes, stirring twice.

5. Add the fish cutlets in a single layer and poach for 5–8 minutes until just cooked through. Lift out on to a warm serving dish and keep hot.

6. Blend the cornflour smoothly with the water, vinegar and egg. Add to the sauce with the chutney, stir round and bring just up to the boil. Simmer gently for 1 minute then spoon over the fish. Garnish each piece with a lemon wedge.

MACHI PULLAU

KEDGEREE INDIAN-STYLE

A *basic and uncomplicated fish and rice dish from the west coast which makes a light but nutritious main course with chutney and either vegetable curry or a leafy green salad. Obviously fish available in Britain has had to be substituted for some of the more flamboyant and exotic oriental varieties, but I can't see anyone complaining too much about haddock and salmon.*

Serves 4

675 g	mixed fish fillets	1½ lb
	such as haddock and salmon, skinned	
30 ml	oil	2 tbsp
	2 onions, grated	
60 ml	desiccated (shredded) coconut	4 tbsp
15 ml	ground coriander (cilantro)	1 tbsp
15 ml	ground cumin	1 tbsp
2.5 ml	turmeric	½ tsp
2.5 ml	ground fenugreek	½ tsp
	3 pinches of ground ginger	
30 ml	lemon juice	2 tbsp
350 g	basmati rice	12 oz/1½ cups
7.5 ml	salt	1½ tsp
750 ml	boiling water	1¼ pt/3 cups
15 ml	oil	1 tbsp
10 ml	fennel seeds	2 tsp

1. Wash and dry the fish then cut into fairly large cubes. Leave aside in a cool place.

2. Pour the oil into a shallow, flameproof, lidded casserole. Heat gently until it just begins to sizzle.

3. Add the onions and fry gently until light golden brown.

4. Stir in the coconut and lightly fry, stirring. Add all the spices with the lemon juice, rice, salt and boiling water. Bring to the boil, cover tightly and cook without looking for 10 minutes.

5. Fork round. Add the fish, re-cover and heat gently for about 5 minutes or until the fish is cooked through.

6. Just before serving, briefly heat the oil and fennel seeds together in a separate small pan. Spoon over the fish and serve straight away.

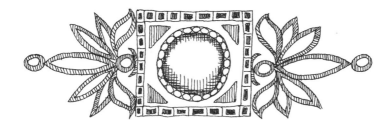

DAHI MACHI

FISH IN COCONUT SAUCE

*T*his is a recipe from eastern India for which you can use
haddock, sole or salmon.
Serves 4

	1 large onion, sliced	
	1 clove garlic, sliced	
2.5 cm	piece fresh ginger, peeled and sliced	1 in
15 ml	oil	1 tbsp
5 ml	ground cumin	1 tsp
5 ml	ground coriander (cilantro)	1 tsp
5 ml	garam masala	1 tsp
2.5 ml	turmeric	½ tsp
1.25 ml	chilli powder	¼ tsp
60 ml	instant coconut powder	4 tbsp
150 ml	warm water	¼ pt/⅔ cup
5 ml	salt	1 tsp
450 g	haddock, sole or salmon, skinned and cubed	1 lb

1. Grind the onion, garlic and ginger to a coarse paste then
fry in the oil in a saucepan until pale gold.

2. Add all the ground spices and fry for about 45 seconds,
then splash in a few drops of cold water to stop the mixture from
burning.

3. Blend the coconut powder smoothly with the water and
stir into the fried ingredients with the salt.

4. Bring to the boil, stirring. Lower the heat and add the fish.
Cover and cook gently for 7–10 minutes, until the fish is cooked
through.

JINGA KARI

PRAWN CURRY

 nother Anglo-Indian dish, this makes a delicious creamy curry.
Serves 6

	Vegetable curry sauce	
	(see Sabzi Ka Kari, page 128)	
500 g	peeled prawns	1¼ lb
30 ml	lemon juice	2 tbsp
150 ml	thick yoghurt or	¼ pt/⅔ cup
	whipping (heavy) cream	

1. Make the sauce as on page 128.

2. Stir in the prawns and heat through for 3–4 minutes.

3. Stir in the lemon juice and yoghurt or cream and warm through briefly. Serve with rice.

JINGA TIKKA KABABS

KING PRAWN TIKKA KEBABS

The marinade gives the ingredients a reddish-brown colour and the piquant flavour of northern India. It works successfully in a Western oven or barbecue although the real thing is usually baked in a tandoor.

Serves 4

450 g	shelled king prawns	1 lb
150 ml	thick yoghurt	¼ pt/⅔ cup
15 ml	tandoori spice mix	1 tbsp
5 ml	garam masala	1 tsp
15 ml	lemon juice	1 tbsp
5 ml	salt	1 tsp
1 cm fresh ginger, peeled and finely chopped ½ in		
2 cloves garlic, finely chopped		

1. Put the prawns into a bowl.

2. For the marinade, beat yoghurt with the spices, lemon juice and salt. Stir in the ginger and garlic.

3. Spoon over the prawns then toss over and over until they are well coated. Cover and refrigerate for 8–12 hours, turning every 2 hours.

4. Thread on to 4 large or 8 smaller skewers and grill or barbecue for about 15 minutes, turning frequently and brushing with any leftover marinade. Serve with warm bread.

CHICKEN

MURGH TANDOORI

TANDOORI CHICKEN

*G*arbed in a vivid orangey-red and slightly charred-looking coating, Tandoori chicken is one step beyond roast chicken, a much loved addition to our own poultry repertoire and traditionally cooked in a tandoor or clay oven (page 34) in restaurants specialising in north Indian food from where this recipe originates. In the home, chicken and meat can be 'tandooried' successfully in a conventional oven, on an outdoor barbecue and even in the microwave followed by heat treatment under the grill. You'll be surprised at just how well this recipe works even without a tandoor. As tandoori spice mix is easy to get hold of there's no point in making your own blend. It's less trouble to go out and buy, and all the commercial brands are excellent.

Serves 4 as a main course, or 8 as starter

	8–12 pieces of fleshy chicken	
250 ml	thick yoghurt	8 fl oz/1 cup
30 ml	tandoori spice mix	2 tbsp
10 ml	ground coriander (cilantro)	2 tsp
5 ml	paprika	1 tsp
5 ml	turmeric	1 tsp
15 ml	lemon juice	1 tbsp
7.5 ml	salt	1½ tsp
	1–2 cloves garlic	
	TO SERVE:	
	Shredded lettuce	
	Onion rings	
	Lemon wedges	
	Tomato slices	

1. Wash and dry the chicken then make deep cuts in the flesh with a small sharp knife. Arrange in a single layer in a roasting tin, either non-stick or lined with foil. Brush the foil with oil.

2. Mix the yoghurt with all the spices then work in the lemon juice. Crush the salt and garlic cloves together in a little dish with the back of a teaspoon. Add to the yoghurt mixture.

3. Spread the mixture thickly over the chicken, getting right inside the cuts. Cover loosely with foil and marinate for 8–10 hours in the refrigerator. Bring back to room temperature before finishing.

4. To cook, remove the foil and roast for 45–60 minutes in a preheated oven at 180°C/350°F/gas 4. When ready, parts of the chicken will look charred. If still not cooked through, re-cover with foil and roast for a further 20 minutes.

5. Arrange on plates lined with shredded lettuce. Garnish with uncooked onion rings, wedges of lemon and tomato slices. Serve with bread.

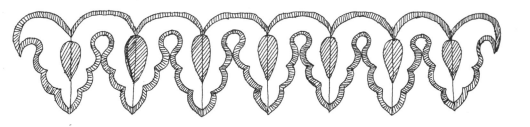

MAKHANI MURGH

BUTTER CHICKEN

restaurant classic and justifiably expensive, this is one of the most opulent recipes in the book and is made from freshly cooked tandoori chicken joints reheated in tomato sauce laden with butter and cream. Serve with bread and a piquant pickle such as shop-bought lime or lemon or even garlic pickle which leaves no aftertaste whatsoever.

Serves 4–6

1 large onion, finely chopped		
1 clove garlic, finely chopped		
1 cm fresh ginger, peeled and finely chopped ½ in		
75 g	butter	3 oz/⅓ cup
15 ml	ground cumin	1 tbsp
5 ml	EACH, ginger, paprika and chilli powder	1 tsp
10 ml	garam masala	2 tsp
2.5 ml	ground fenugreek	½ tsp
30 ml	tomato purée (paste)	2 tbsp
5 ml	sugar	1 tsp
5 ml	salt	1 tsp
6 tomatoes, skinned and chopped		
Juice of ½ lime or lemon		
8 joints freshly cooked Tandoori Chicken (see page 70)		
150 ml	double (heavy) cream ¼ pt/⅔ cup	
60 ml chopped fresh coriander (cilantro) 4 tbsp		

1. Fry the onion, garlic and ginger in the butter in a pan until light gold.

2. Stir in all the spices followed by the tomato purée, sugar and salt. Add the tomatoes and lime or lemon juice. Leave over a low heat.

3. Divide the chicken joints into small, neat pieces and add to the tomato mixture. Simmer, half-covered, for 20 minutes until chicken is well heated through. Keep over a gentle heat.

4. Gradually blend in the cream, stir round gently with a spoon and reheat briefly. Serve each portion sprinkled with coriander.

MURGH TIKKA KABABS

CHICKEN TIKKA KEBABS

raditionally baked in a tandoor, these reddish-brown kebabs from northern India work just as successfully in a Western oven or barbecue and do bear a likeness to the real thing. As it marinates, the chicken develops a melt-in-the-mouth tenderness, is piquantly flavoured and could turn out to be a dinner party classic, appealing to all. Garnish serving plates with thin rings of fresh onion, wedges of tomato, slices of lime and shredded lettuce.

Serves 4

450 g	boneless chicken breast	1 lb
150 ml	thick yoghurt	¼ pt/⅔ cup
15 ml	tandoori spice mix	1 tbsp
5 ml	garam masala	1 tsp
15 ml	lemon juice	1 tbsp
5 ml	salt	1 tsp
1 cm	fresh ginger, peeled and finely chopped	½ in
	2 cloves garlic, finely chopped	

1. Wash and dry the chicken, removing the skin. Cut the flesh into bite-sized pieces and put into a basin.

2. For the marinade, beat the yoghurt with the spices, lemon juice and salt. Stir in the ginger and garlic.

3. Spoon over the chicken then toss over and over until the pieces are well coated. Cover and refrigerate for 8–12 hours, turning every 2 hours.

4. Thread on to 4 large or 8 smaller skewers and grill or barbecue for about 15 minutes, turning frequently and brushing with any leftover marinade. Serve with warm bread.

BENGAL MURGH TALI

FRIED CHICKEN WITH GINGER

*I*nstead of including sugar, as is usual in this sweetish Bengali fried chicken from the north-east, I have substituted two ingredients: ginger syrup and preserved stem ginger instead of fresh. The whole thing works magnificently. The chicken turns deep golden brown and lustrous and the flavour is agreeably sweet without being cloying. If you have a wok, use it to stir-fry the chicken.

Serves 4

	8 chicken portions	
30 ml	oil	2 tbsp
	1 large onion, chopped	
	2 cloves garlic, chopped	
	2 green chillies, deseeded	
	4 knobs preserved ginger in syrup, sliced	
60 ml	ginger syrup	4 tbsp
150 ml	hot water	¼ pt/⅔ cup
5 ml	salt	1 tsp

1. Skin, wash and dry each portion of chicken. Stir-fry in the oil in a large frying pan or wok until the chicken is well browned on all sides. Leave the pan uncovered and fry for a further 15–20 minutes over a moderate heat; too high and the chicken will burn.

2. Meanwhile, grind together the onion, garlic, chillies and preserved ginger.

3. Add to the chicken and mix in well. Stir in the syrup, water and salt.

4. Cover and continue to simmer steadily for 15 minutes, stirring and turning the chicken several times. Finally, uncover and cook for 3 minutes. Serve straight away with potatoes and/or vegetables of your choice.

MURGH PAKORA

SPICED FRIED CHICKEN IN BESAN FLOUR

nother northern recipe, this fried chicken is in a league of its own with a crunchy, spicy coating and warm golden brown colour. Eat it with Dhokla (see page 46), a potato dish and sweet chutney. Although still traditional, I have simplified the method to save time and effort.

Serves 6–8

1 large roasting chicken, oven-ready		
75 g	besan or gram flour	3 oz/¾ cup
7.5 ml	salt	1½ tsp
60 ml	oil	4 tbsp
3 cloves garlic, chopped		
2.5 cm	fresh ginger, peeled and chopped	1 in
1–3 green chillies, to taste, deseeded		
10 ml	ghee	2 tsp
10 ml	garam masala	2 tsp
5 ml	ground coriander (cilantro)	1 tsp
45 ml	malt vinegar	3 tbsp

1. Divide the chicken into small portions, boning out the breast. Wash well then wipe dry with kitchen paper.

2. Sift the gram flour and salt on to a large piece of foil. Add the chicken and toss over and over until all the pieces are well coated.

3. Heat the oil in a large frying pan until really hot. Add the chicken and fry fairly briskly until golden brown, turning 2 or 3 times. Lower the heat slightly and continue to fry, uncovered, for a total of 20 minutes, turning twice more.

4. Grind the garlic, ginger and chillies to a paste and scrape into a separate small pan. Add the ghee and fry gently for about 3 minutes. Mix in the spices and vinegar (the aroma will be quite strong for a few seconds) then use to coat the chicken.

5. Continue to fry, covered, a little more gently, for another 20–25 minutes or when it is obvious that the chicken is well cooked through and tender.

6. Turn over about 3 times then drain on a plate lined with crumpled kitchen paper. Serve hot.

MURGH MUSALLAM

MARINATED WHOLE CHICKEN

A spectacular chicken dish originally from the Mogul Empire in the north, this is one of the grandest and most regal in the whole sub-continent. The reason why restaurants ask for advance notice is because, properly prepared, the chicken has to be left to marinate for around 8 hours before being cooked. Recipes for it abound, all different, but the one thing they have in common is the spicy yoghurt marinade which converts automatically into a glorious cooking sauce. Some cooks tell you to leave the chicken alone and unfilled, others to stuff the neck area with a customary Indian stuffing combination: rice, hard-boiled eggs and peas. Either way it's superb but labour-intensive.

Serves 6–8

	1 medium to large roasting chicken, left whole but skinned	
	MARINADE:	
150 ml	yoghurt	¼ pt/⅔ cup
	Seeds from 4 green cardamom pods	
2.5 cm	cinnamon stick	1 in
	3 cloves	
	2 dried red chillies	
15 ml	coriander (cilantro) seeds	1 tbsp
5 ml	cumin seeds	1 tsp
5 ml	salt	1 tsp
	STUFFING:	
75 g	basmati rice	3 oz/⅓ cup
250 ml	cold water	8 fl oz/1 cup
5 ml	salt	1 tsp
	2 hard-boiled eggs	
50 g	frozen peas	2 oz/½ cup
30 ml	seedless raisins	2 tbsp

SAUCE OR MASALA:		
1 large onion, chopped		
2 cloves garlic, chopped		
1 cm	fresh ginger, peeled and chopped	½ in
2 medium green chillies, deseeded and chopped		
30 ml	oil	2 tbsp
10 ml	dark poppy seeds	2 tsp
30 ml	ground almonds	2 tbsp
10 ml	ground cumin	2 tsp
5 ml	turmeric	1 tsp
5 ml	ground coriander (cilantro)	1 tsp
150 ml	yoghurt	¼ pt/⅔ cup
150 ml	water	¼ pt/⅔ cup
10 ml	salt	2 tsp

Chopped fresh coriander (cilantro) to garnish

1. Wash the chicken inside and out and wipe dry with kitchen paper. Place in a large dish.

2. Spoon the yoghurt into a small mixing bowl. Finely grind all the spices together and stir into yoghurt with the salt.

3. Spread all over the chicken, cover loosely with greaseproof or parchment paper and marinate in the refrigerator for 8 hours. Turn 3 times.

4. Prepare the stuffing. Rinse the rice thoroughly, put into a saucepan and add the water and salt. Cover closely and boil for 10 minutes. Fork round to separate the grains and cool.

5. To complete, shell and quarter the eggs and mix into the rice with the remaining stuffing ingredients.

6. Lift the chicken out of its marinade and transfer to a large flameproof casserole. Pack the stuffing carefully into the neck end with a spoon.

7. To make the sauce, fry the onion, garlic, ginger and chillies in the oil in a saucepan until light gold. Add the poppy seeds, almonds and spices and fry slowly for 4 minutes, stirring. Mix in any leftover marinade with yoghurt, water and salt and simmer a further 5 minutes.

8. Pour the sauce over the chicken. Cover the casserole securely with its lid and cook chicken over a very low heat for 1¼ hours. Have a look every so often and top up with a little extra water if the liquid seems to be drying out.

9. Carve the chicken into neat portions, arrange on warm plates and coat with the sauce. Sprinkle each serving with the coriander.

MURGH SIMLA

CHICKEN SIMLA

hades of the past, of the British in Poona in western India, the Raj, the lasting Anglo-Indian culinary connection, days gone by but still remembered.

Serves 6

	1 chicken, freshly roasted	
	1 clove garlic, finely chopped	
1 cm	fresh ginger, finely chopped	½ in
30 ml	oil	2 tbsp
2.5 ml	turmeric	½ tsp
2.5 ml	paprika	½ tsp
7.5 ml	salt	1½ tsp
300 ml	double (heavy) cream	½ pt/1¼ cups

1. Divide the chicken into 6 neat pieces and arrange over the base of a heatproof serving dish. Keep warm.

2. Fry the garlic and ginger in the oil in a saucepan until pale gold. Stir in the turmeric and paprika and fry a further 40 seconds.

3. Stir in the salt and cream. Bring the mixture to the boil, stirring constantly. Pour over the chicken. Reheat and brown for 15 minutes in a preheated oven at 200°C/400°F/gas 6. Serve with rice and chutney.

MURGH NIZAM

CHICKEN NIZAM

A celebration of luxury and riches and originally created for the mega-wealthy Nizam of Hyderabad in central India. Certainly chicken cooked this way is fit for any emperor's feast and it could be classed as medium hot.

Serves 6

	6 boned chicken breasts	
	1 large onion, chopped	
	2 cloves garlic, chopped	
2.5 cm	fresh ginger, peeled and chopped	1 in
	2 green chillies, deseeded and chopped	
	1 dried red chilli	
15 ml	poppy seeds	1 tbsp
30 ml	oil	2 tbsp
10 ml	ground cumin	2 tsp
10 ml	garam masala	2 tsp
60 ml	instant coconut milk powder	4 tbsp
250 ml	warm water	8 fl oz/1 cup
5 ml	salt	1 tsp
15 ml	chopped fresh coriander (cilantro)	1 tbsp
	pinch of ground saffron	
45 ml	desiccated (shredded) coconut	3 tbsp
150 ml	thick yoghurt	¼ pt/⅔ cup

1. Skin and wash the chicken. Wipe dry with kitchen paper, then cut flesh into fairly small cubes.

2. Grind the onion, garlic, ginger, green chillies, red chilli and poppy seeds to a paste.

3. Fry in a fairly large saucepan in the oil until light gold. Mix in the cumin and garam masala and fry for 40 seconds, splashing in a little cold water to prevent the herbs from burning.

4. Add the chicken flesh and stir round in the spice mixture. Blend the coconut powder and water smoothly together and pour into the saucepan. Bring to the boil, stirring, lower the heat and cover.

5. Simmer gently for 45–60 minutes or until the chicken is tender. Finally add the rest of the ingredients and stir until smooth over a low heat. Serve with plain boiled rice and a vegetable curry.

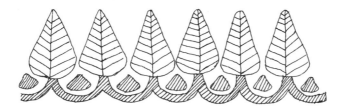

MURGH MOGHLAI

MAJESTIC CHICKEN

he northern version of the Murgh Nizam from Uttar Pradesh is equally rich, and with similar ingredients. It has flair, majesty and elegance and requires nothing more than Indian bread by way of accompaniment – and Indian champagne if the mood is right.

Serves 6

2.5 ml	saffron strands	½ tsp
30 ml	hot water	2 tbsp
	1 onion, chopped	
	1 clove garlic, chopped	
1 cm	fresh ginger, peeled and chopped	½ in
	1 dried red chilli, deseeded	
15 ml	dark poppy seeds	1 tbsp
50 g	flaked almonds	2 oz/½ cup
45 ml	desiccated (shredded) coconut	3 tbsp
30 ml	oil	2 tbsp
15 ml	mild korma curry powder	1 tbsp
5 ml	ground cumin	1 tsp
5 ml	garam masala	1 tsp
1 kg	tender chicken pieces	2 lb
300 ml	full cream milk	½ pt/1¼ cups
7.5 ml	salt	1½ tsp
150 ml	thick yoghurt	¼ pt/⅔ cup

1. Soak the saffron in the hot water for about 10 minutes.

2. Grind together the onion, garlic, ginger, chilli, poppy seeds, almonds and coconut to a fairly coarse paste.

3. Fry in a large saucepan in the oil until light golden brown. Mix in the curry powder, cumin and garam masala, then stir in the chicken pieces.

THE INDIAN RED

641.5954 ALLISON

4. Pour in the milk, add the salt and bring slowly to the boil, stirring continually.

5. Lower the heat and cover. Simmer gently for 1¼ hours or until the chicken is tender, stirring occasionally.

6. Gradually mix in the yoghurt, reheat briefly and serve.

MURGH TIKKA MASALA

CHICKEN TIKKA MASALA

ow on supermarket shelves as well as on restaurant menus, the chicken in this stunning dish from northern India is cocooned in a delicate, spicy sauce and has become a star attraction with lovers of mild Indian food. Serve with rice or bread and any of the vegetables from the vegetable section.

Serves 6

1 kg	boned chicken breast	2 lb
	1 large onion, chopped	
	2 cloves garlic, chopped	
1 cm	fresh ginger, peeled and chopped	½ in
	1 green chilli, deseeded	
	5 fresh mint leaves	
30 ml	lime or lemon juice	2 tbsp
150 ml	thick yoghurt	¼ pt/⅔ cup
15 ml	oil	1 tbsp
10 ml	paprika	2 tsp
10 ml	garam masala	2 tsp
	Large pinch of grated nutmeg	
5 ml	turmeric	1 tsp
30 ml	tomato purée (paste)	2 tbsp
7.5 ml	salt	1½ tsp

1. Skin the chicken, wash and pat dry then cut flesh into bite-sized pieces.

2. Grind together the onion, garlic, ginger, chilli and mint leaves to a fairly coarse paste.

3. Beat in the lime or lemon juice and all the remaining ingredients. Add the chicken, toss over and over gently with a spoon until each piece is well coated with the yoghurt mixture, then cover the bowl tightly with cling film. Refrigerate overnight.

4. To cook, transfer the bowl contents to a saucepan. Bring gently to the boil, stirring. Lower the heat and cover.

5. Simmer for about 45 minutes or until the chicken is tender, stirring from time to time to prevent sticking.

TIP
To make the masala even richer, add another 150 ml/¼ pt/⅔ cup of yoghurt and 30 ml/2 tbsp of ground almonds just before serving, heating through until smooth.

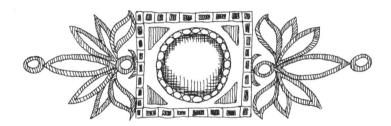

MURGH KORMA

CHICKEN KORMA

*K*orma cooking from the north is a gentle giant, creamy and
rich-tasting, mildly spiced and delicate, exquisitely balanced with
ground almonds – flaked almonds as well sometimes - and the thickest
yoghurt you can find. In Indian homes it is always accompanied by
bread, never rice, although in the West there are no hard and fast rules
and the choice remains a personal one. To cut down on the long list of
spice ingredients customarily used in India, I have opted for korma
curry powder and garam masala instead as, between the two, they
contain most of the spices an Indian cook would use.
Serves 4

2.5 ml	saffron strands	½ tsp
30 ml	boiling water	2 tbsp
450-500 g	boned chicken breasts	1-1¼ lb
15 ml	oil	1 tbsp
15 ml	vegetable or butter ghee	1 tbsp
	(or use concentrated butter)	
	1 onion, grated	
	2 cloves garlic, crushed	
5 ml	garam masala	1 tsp
10 ml	korma curry powder	2 tsp
	Seeds from 6 green cardamom pods	
	1 bay leaf	
300 ml	boiling water	½ pt/1¼ cups
60 ml	ground almonds	4 tbsp
5 ml	salt	1 tsp
150 ml	thick yoghurt	¼ pt/⅔ cup

GARNISH:		
60 ml	flaked almonds, lightly toasted	4 tbsp

1. Soak the saffron in boiling water while preparing rest of dish.

2. Wash the chicken, pat dry with paper towels and cut into narrow strips.

3. Sizzle oil and ghee together in a pan, add the onion and garlic and fry gently until light gold. Add the spices and continue to fry gently for 3 minutes. Add a splash of cold water to prevent spices from burning.

4. Mix in the chicken strips and stir-fry until the colour changes from pink to beige. This should take 3–4 minutes.

5. Add water, almonds and salt. Bring slowly to the boil. Cover and simmer over a low heat for 20 minutes.

6. Stir in the yoghurt, warm through then spoon into a serving dish. Garnish with flaked almonds.

PALEK MURGH

CHICKEN AND SPINACH

This is a northern recipe. Follow the recipe for Palek Gosht on page 108, substituting diced chicken breast for lamb.
Serves 4–5

MURGH PASSANDA

CHICKEN PASSANDA

Follow the recipe for Passanda Gosht on page 106, substituting diced chicken breast for lamb, to create another delicious curry from Hyderabad.
Serves 6–8

MURGH KARI

CHICKEN CURRY

*T**his is a popular dish throughout India and makes a simple and delicious meal.*

Serves 6

	Vegetable curry sauce	
	(see Sabzi Ka Kari, page 128)	
	6 chicken portions, skinned	
	salt	
30 ml	coconut milk.	2 tbsp

1. Make the sauce as described on page 128.

2. Add the chicken portions, bring to the boil, cover and simmer for 1 hour until the chicken is tender.

3. Season to taste with salt and stir in the coconut milk. Warm through before serving with rice.

MURGH JALFREZI

CHICKEN JALFREZI

A fried chicken and vegetable combo, believed to be British in origin from the north. It is a fairly hot and spicy dish, quite dry and tinted orange with tomato purée. Another which is generally served with bread, it calls for bowls of yoghurt or raita and a sweet chutney to calm the throat.

Serves 4

	12 fleshy chicken drumsticks	
45 ml	oil	3 tbsp
	2 large onions, finely chopped	
	2 cloves garlic, finely chopped	
2.5 cm	fresh ginger, peeled and finely chopped	1 in
	1 red (bell) pepper, deseeded and cut into strips	
	1 green (bell) pepper, deseeded and cut into strips	
	2 green chillies, deseeded and cut into strips	
10 ml	garam masala	2 tsp
15 ml	medium hot curry powder	1 tbsp
2.5 ml	chilli powder (optional)	1 tsp
15 ml	desiccated (shredded) coconut	1 tbsp
30 ml	tomato purée (paste)	2 tbsp
45 ml	cold water	3 tbsp
10 ml	salt	2 tsp

GARNISH:

Crisply fried onion rings and/or
chopped fresh coriander (cilantro)

1. Skin, wash and dry drumsticks, then make deepish cuts in the flesh as this helps the flavours to penetrate.

2. Heat the oil in a pan and fry the onions, garlic, ginger, peppers and chillies over a low heat until light gold. Add the spices and coconut and continue to fry gently for 3–4 minutes, stirring.

3. Whisk the remaining ingredients well together. Add to pan with the chicken.

4. Bring slowly to the boil, lower the heat and cover. Simmer gently for about 45 minutes or until the chicken is tender. Sprinkle each portion with onion rings and coriander.

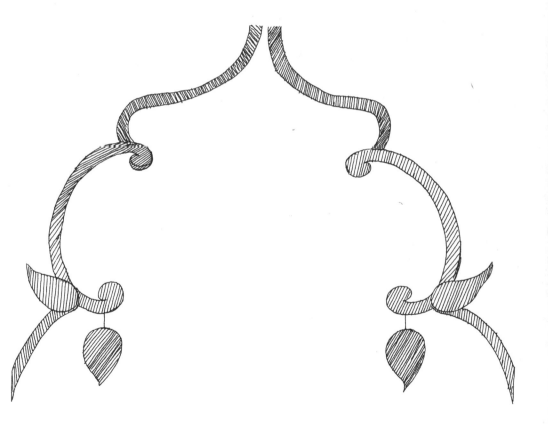

MURGH DO-PIAZA

CHICKEN DO-PIAZA

*o means two and piaza is the word for onions in this recipe
from Uttar Pradesh. Put them together and, depending on the
book you happen to be following, it can mean: twice the amount of
onions to chicken or meat; onions added at two stages during cooking;
two-thirds of the onions added early on and the last third fried and used
as a garnish. I have opted for the last method because it tastes and looks
more appetising than the other two. It is medium hot.*

Serves 6

4 large onions, thinly sliced into rings		
50 g	ghee	2 oz/¼ cup
10 ml	oil	2 tsp
675 g	boned chicken breast	1½ lb
2.5 cm	fresh ginger, peeled and finely chopped	1 in
2 cloves garlic, finely chopped		
2 green chillies, deseeded		
4 cloves		
2.5 cm	cinnamon stick	1 in
6 green cardamom pods, bruised with knife handle or hammer		
15 ml	cumin seeds	1 tbsp
1 blade mace or 3–4 pinches of grated nutmeg		
10 ml	turmeric	2 tsp
10 ml	salt	2 tsp
150 ml	thick yoghurt	¼ pt/⅔ cup
45 ml	chopped fresh coriander (cilantro)	3 tbsp
150 ml	cold water	¼ pt/⅔ cup

1. Fry the onion rings gently in the ghee and oil in a large
pan until deep gold, allowing about 15 minutes. Remove about one-
third and keep aside.

2. Skin, wash and dry the chicken then cut into dice. Add to pan and stir round with the onions.

3. Add the ginger, garlic and chillies and fry gently until pale gold. Add all the spices with the salt, yoghurt, half the coriander and the water.

4. Bring to the boil, stirring. Lower the heat and cover. Simmer gently for 45 minutes, topping up with a trace of water every now and then if the liquid seems to be drying out too much. Stir occasionally.

5. To serve, dust the reserved onions with a little flour and re-fry without additional ghee or oil until crisp. Sprinkle over each portion of the chicken with remaining coriander.

MURGH DHANSAK

CHICKEN DHANSAK

*W*arm and sweet-sour and originally brought to India from Persia, the Dhansak is fairly hot, glowing marigold yellow and resembles a fairly hearty stew with lentils. Serve it with bread, chutney and raita (page 162) to taste.

Serves 6

	6 boned chicken breasts	
	1 large onion, finely chopped	
	2 cloves garlic, finely chopped	
	2 green chillies, deseeded and finely chopped	
2.5 cm	fresh ginger, peeled and finely chopped	1 in
30 ml	oil	2 tbsp
7.5 ml	chilli powder	1½ tsp
10 ml	garam masala	2 tsp
10 ml	ground coriander (cilantro)	2 tsp
10 ml	cumin	2 tsp
5 ml	turmeric	1 tsp
175 g	orange lentils	6 oz/1 cup
10 ml	salt	2 tsp
600 ml	cold water	1 pt/2½ cups
	Juice of 1 large lemon	
45 ml	malt vinegar	3 tbsp
	2 large potatoes, diced	
	4 tomatoes, skinned and chopped	
	4 cloves	
	Chopped fresh coriander (cilantro) to garnish	

1. Skin chicken, wash and dry the flesh and cut into small cubes.

2. Fry the onion, garlic, chillies and ginger in the oil in a large saucepan until pale gold. Add the chicken and continue to fry until it loses its raw look.

3. Add all the spices, rinsed lentils, salt, water, lemon juice and vinegar. Add the potatoes with tomatoes and cloves and mix in thoroughly.

4. Bring to the boil, stirring. Lower the heat and cover. Continue to simmer gently until the potatoes and lentils are well cooked down, about 1–1½ hours. Stir frequently. Sprinkle each portion with coriander.

MURGH MADRAS

CHICKEN MADRAS

A *hot and brow-mopping curry, developed by restaurant chefs in the south of India to please their non-vegetarian clients who are passionate about fiery food. Plain boiled rice is a great solace, as are cooling bowls of raitas and diced cucumber and tomato – and a fruity chutney as well for good measure. If you like, you can garnish the curry with sliced hard-boiled egg.*

Serves 4–6

	12 fleshy chicken thighs	
30 ml	oil	2 tbsp
	2 onions, finely chopped	
	2 cloves garlic, finely chopped	
2.5 cm	fresh ginger, finely chopped	1 in
15 ml	garam masala	1 tbsp
45 ml	medium or hot	3 tbsp
	Madras curry powder	
	1 bay leaf	
75 ml	instant coconut milk powder	5 tbsp
300 ml	warm water	½ pt/1¼ cups
5 ml	salt	1 tsp

1. Skin the chicken then wash and dry with kitchen paper.

2. Heat the oil in a pan, add the chicken and fry briskly until well browned all over, turning once or twice. Remove to a plate.

3. Add the onions, garlic and ginger to the remaining oil in the pan and fry until light gold. Mix in the spices and fry slowly for about 2 minutes, stirring all the time.

4. Combine the coconut powder smoothly with the water. Pour into the pan and stir over medium heat until bubbles just begin to break on the surface.

5. Stir in the salt, replace the chicken and turn over and over in the coconut sauce. Reduce the heat, cover the pan and simmer gently for 1 hour or until chicken is tender, stirring from time to time.

MURGH VINDALOO

CHICKEN VINDALOO

Vindaloo is a speciality of Goa. Follow the recipe for Gosht Vindaloo on page 122, substituting diced raw chicken or turkey breast for the pork. Cook for only 45 minutes before adding the potatoes.
Serves 4 ·

MURGH XACUTI

CHICKEN XACUTI

blisteringly hot and chocolate dark curry from in and around Goa, this is regularly served to diners in an Indian restaurant in the centre of Bath. If you make it at home, eat with caution and ensure you have cooling raitas or yoghurt to hand to pass round. Serve plenty of rice, too, and maybe some dhal.

Serves 6

30 ml	dark poppy seeds	2 tbsp
2.5 ml	whole fenugreek	½ tsp
Seeds from 8 black cardamom pods		
2-6 dried red chillies		
5 ml	turmeric	1 tsp
60 ml	desiccated (shredded) coconut	4 tbsp
12-18 skinned chicken thighs		
45 ml	oil	3 tbsp
2 onions, finely chopped		
2 cloves garlic, finely chopped		
2.5 cm fresh ginger, peeled and finely chopped 1 in		
45 ml	lemon juice	3 tbsp
150 ml	hot water	¼ pt/⅔ cup
7.5 ml	salt	1½ tsp

1. In a heavy frying pan, dry roast all the spices with the coconut for about 1–1½ minutes until you can smell their fragrance. Keep the heat medium to prevent scorching and stir all the time.

2. Cool completely then grind fairly finely in a food processor or grinder.

3. Wash and dry the chicken and fry briskly in a saucepan with the oil until golden and crisp all over, turning frequently. Transfer to a plate.

4. Add the onions, garlic and ginger to the pan containing the oil and fry gently, stirring until light gold.

5. Stir in the spice and coconut mixture, replace the chicken and add all remaining ingredients.

6. Bring to the boil, lower the heat and cover. Simmer for about 45 minutes until the chicken is cooked through, stirring occasionally.

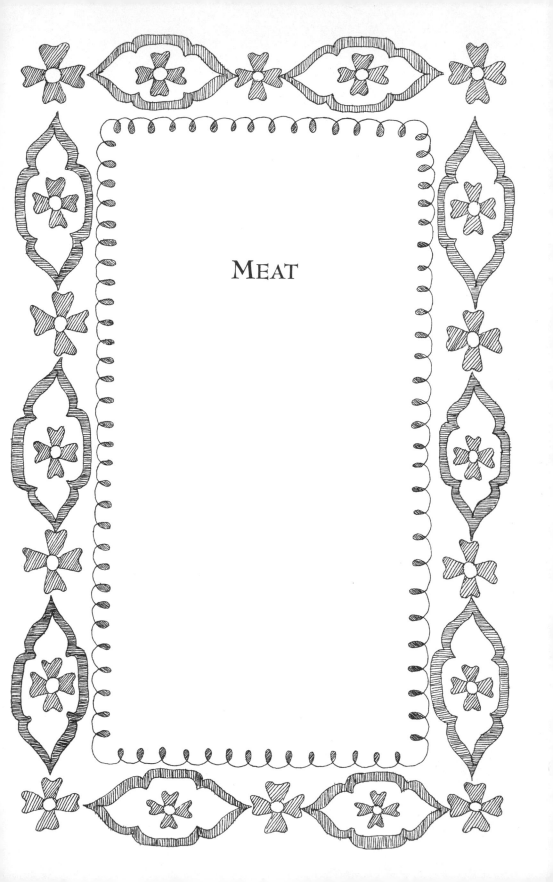

MEAT

BHOONA GOSHT

DRY LAMB CURRY

A dryish fried curry from the north (bhoona means fried) which is medium hot and speckled with coconut. It is a convivial contribution, often seen on restaurant menus, and generally eaten with bread. To accompany, choose a moist vegetable dish from the vegetable section plus one or two raitas and chutney.

Serves 4

675 g	lamb fillet	1½ lb
	1 onion, chopped	
	2 cloves garlic, chopped	
2.5 cm	fresh ginger, peeled and chopped	1 in
	1 green chilli, deseeded and chopped	
30 ml	oil	2 tbsp
5 ml	turmeric	1 tsp
5 ml	cinnamon	1 tsp
10 ml	medium hot curry powder	2 tsp
15 ml	garam masala	1 tbsp
15 ml	tomato purée (paste)	1 tbsp
	2 cloves	
30 ml	desiccated (shredded) coconut	2 tbsp
30 ml	malt vinegar	2 tbsp
15 ml	lemon juice	1 tbsp
300 ml	water	½ pt/1¼ cups
7.5 ml	salt	1½ tsp

1. Wash and dry the lamb and cut into small cubes.

2. Grind the onion, garlic, ginger and chilli to a paste.

3. Fry in the oil in a saucepan until light golden brown. Mix in all the spices followed by the lamb. Stir-fry for 5–7 minutes then add all remaining ingredients from tomato purée to salt.

4. Bring to the boil, lower the heat and cover. Simmer gently for 45 minutes, stirring occasionally.

5. Uncover and continue to simmer over a minimal heat until almost no liquid remains, allowing anything from 10–20 minutes.

6. Stir fairly often and add a splash of cold water now and then if the mixture looks over dry. Serve straight away.

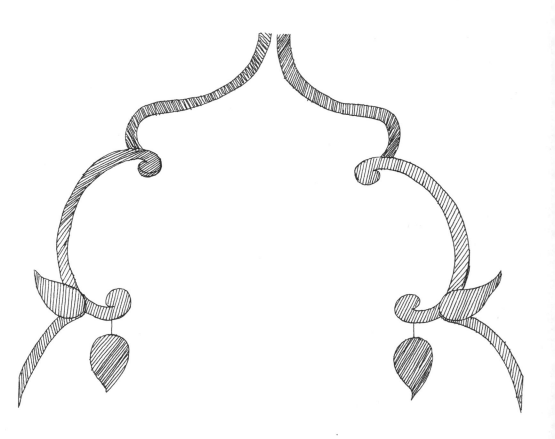

PASSANDA GOSHT

LAMB PASSANDA

*A*lso called Barra Kabab, the name Passanda itself refers to the small slices of lamb from which the dish is made and is a rich, gentle and aristocratic delicacy from Hyderabad, a part of the country noted for its beauty, artistry and culture.

Serves 6–8

1 kg	piece of boned leg of lamb, trimmed of all fat	2 lb
30 ml	oil	2 tbsp
	2 large onions, grated	

MARINADE:

250 ml	thick yoghurt	8 fl oz/1 cup
1 cm	fresh ginger, peeled and chopped	½ in
	2 cloves garlic, crushed	
	1 green chilli, deseeded and chopped	
15 ml	dark poppy seeds	1 tbsp
5 ml	turmeric	1 tsp
10 ml	paprika	2 tsp
5 ml	cinnamon	1 tsp
10 ml	garam masala	2 tsp
10 ml	ground cumin	2 tsp
5 ml	ground coriander (cilantro)	1 tsp
10 ml	salt	2 tsp
30 ml	ground almonds	2 tbsp

GARNISH:

	8 spring onions (scallions), chopped
	2 small green chillies, deseeded and chopped
45 ml	chopped fresh coriander (cilantro) 3 tbsp

1. Cut the meat into thin slices, about the length of a forefinger and 5–8 cm/2–3 in in width. Put into a shallow dish.

2. Heat the oil in a roomy frying pan. Add the onions and fry gently until pale gold. Cover and leave aside.

3. To make the marinade, tip the yoghurt into a bowl. Grind together the ginger, garlic, chilli and poppy seeds. Add to the yoghurt with all the remaining ingredients. Stir thoroughly.

4. Add the lamb slices and toss over and over until each piece is well coated with the marinade. Cover and refrigerate for 3–4 hours.

5. Add to the fried onions in the frying pan. Slowly bring to the boil then cover and simmer gently for 45 minutes, stirring occasionally.

6. Transfer to a serving dish. Sprinkle with the spring onions, chillies and coriander.

PALEK GOSHT

LAMB AND SPINACH

classic from the Punjab in northern India which has been popular in the West for well over fifty years. It is on the dryish side and relatively mild.

Serves 4–6

675 g	neck of lamb fillet	1½ lb
	1 large onion, finely chopped	
	1 clove garlic, finely chopped	
1 cm	fresh ginger, peeled and finely chopped	½ in
15 ml	oil	1 tbsp
5 ml	paprika	1 tsp
5 ml	turmeric	1 tsp
5 ml	ground coriander (cilantro)	1 tsp
15 ml	mild curry powder	1 tbsp
10 ml	ground cumin	2 tsp
2.5 cm	cinnamon stick	1 in
450 g	fresh spinach	1 lb
10 ml	salt	2 tsp

1. Wash and dry the lamb then cut into medium-sized cubes.

2. Fry the onion, garlic and ginger in the oil in a saucepan until pale gold.

3. Mix in all the spices, including the cinnamon stick, and fry over a medium heat for 2 minutes, stirring. Add a splash of cold water to prevent the spices from burning.

4. Add the prepared lamb and stir-fry for 5 minutes. Cover the pan and leave over a low heat while preparing the spinach.

5. Wash the leaves carefully to remove grit but leave wet. Coarsely chop and add to the pan with the salt.

6. Slowly bring to the boil, stirring. Lower the heat and cover. Cook gently for 45 minutes then uncover and continue to simmer until most of the liquid has evaporated, stirring often. Serve with rice or bread, a salad to taste, chutney and raita.

SHAMI KABABS

MINCED LAMB KEBABS

*T*hese could best be described as Indian hamburgers from Uttar
Pradesh since they are also eaten in or with bread and dolloped
with mint chutney instead of the obligatory tomato ketchup. They make
a welcome change from other minced meat dishes, as do the Shahi
Kababs below. The main difference between the two is that the first ones
are round and the second, elongated. Additionally, the spices are slightly
different. Serve with sliced onions, sliced tomatoes and wedges of lemon.
   Serves 4

15 g	fresh coriander (cilantro) leaves, loosely packed	½ oz/ 1 cup
	2 cloves garlic	
5 ml	cumin seeds	1 tsp
	Seeds from 4 green cardamon pods	
2.5 ml	ground ginger	½ tsp
5 cm	cinnamon stick	2 in
10 ml	dark poppy seeds	2 tsp
2.5 ml	chilli powder	½ tsp
450 g	lean minced (ground) lamb	1 lb

1. Finely grind together all the ingredients except the meat.

2. Combine smoothly with the lamb then shape into 8 round
and flattish cakes with damp hands. Cover loosely with foil.

3. Refrigerate for 3–4 hours then dry-fry in a non-stick frying
pan, allowing 7–8 minutes cooking time and turning once.

SHAHI KABABS

LAMB KEBABS WITH YOGHURT

*S*imilar to the Shamis but with a different shape, these are sometimes threaded on to skewers and grilled, but I found the pieces of meat tended to break up and the kebabs were much better behaved when grilled on their own, and also easier to turn.

Follow the recipe for the Shami Kababs but add 30 ml/2 tbsp yoghurt and the same amount of brown flour to the lamb with all the ground spices plus 2.5 ml/½ tsp garam masala. Shape into 8 oblongs which should resemble fat cigars with pointed ends. Cover loosely with foil and refrigerate for 3–4 hours. Grill for 8–10 minutes, turning twice.

SEEKH KABABS

LAMB KEBABS WITH MINT

A Turkish variant much enjoyed in India, follow the exact recipe for the Shami Kababs but add 5 ml/1 tsp mint sauce with all the other ingredients.

KOFTA KABAB

LAMB KEBAB

An easy approach to a traditional and mild Punjabi meatball curry set in a vivacious orangey-brown sauce. Serve with bread, pickles and salad.

Serves 4

	2 large onions	
5 ml	garlic salt	1 tsp
450 g	lean minced (ground) lamb	1 lb
2.5 ml	chilli powder	½ tsp
2.5 ml	ground ginger	½ tsp
2.5 ml	cinnamon	½ tsp
	1 beaten egg	
5 ml	salt	1 tsp
30 ml	oil	2 tbsp
150 ml	boiling water	¼ pt/⅔ cup
15 ml	tomato purée (paste)	1 tbsp
5 ml	ground cumin	1 tsp
5 ml	ground coriander (cilantro)	1 tsp
5 ml	turmeric	1 tsp
5 ml	medium Madras curry powder	1 tsp
5 ml	sugar	1 tsp
5 ml	extra salt	1 tsp
15 ml	chopped fresh mint	1 tbsp

1. Finely grate 1 onion. Transfer to a bowl and work in the next 7 ingredients with your hands.

2. When well combined, shape into 30 small balls, cover loosely with foil and refrigerate for 20 minutes.

3. Fry in hot oil in a large frying pan until well browned all over then remove temporarily to a plate.

4. Finely chop the second peeled onion and add to the pan with all remaining ingredients.

5. Slowly bring to the boil, stirring all the time. Replace the meatballs. Leave uncovered and simmer gently for 25 minutes. Turn over 2–3 times.

KEEMA MATAR

MINCED LAMB CURRY WITH PEAS

A savoury mince from the Punjab without going over the top heatwise, this is another recipe which calls for bread – Indians use it for scooping up the meat – but you can compromise and use rice instead. It goes well with some of the hotter pickles such as lime.
Serves 4–6

	1 large onion, finely chopped	
	1 clove garlic, finely chopped	
2.5 cm	fresh ginger, peeled and chopped	1 in
15 ml	oil	1 tbsp
	1 dried red chilli	
	4 cloves	
	1 bay leaf	
5 ml	turmeric	1 tsp
	Seeds from 4 green cardamom pods	
10 ml	garam masala	2 tsp
7.5 ml	salt	1½ tsp
450 g	lean minced (ground) lamb	1 lb
450 ml	cold water	¾ pt/2 cups
350 g	frozen peas	12 oz/3 cups
150 g	thick yoghurt	¼ pt/⅔ cup

1. Grind the onion, garlic and ginger to a paste and fry in the oil in a saucepan until pale gold.

2. Stir in all the spices from the chilli to garam masala and salt. Fry for about 2 minutes, stirring, then add a splash of cold water to stop the spices from burning.

3. Stir in the minced lamb and fry for 5 minutes, breaking it up with a fork all the time. Add the water and bring to the boil.

4. Lower the heat and cover. Simmer gently for 30 minutes, stirring from time to time.

5. Uncover and continue to simmer for a further 20 minutes. Add the peas and yoghurt and heat through for 7 minutes, stirring occasionally.

GOSHT ROGAN JOSH

LAMB AND TOMATO CURRY

A medium hot lamb and tomato stew from Kashmir in the north, which is gently simmered with a classic blend of spices and thickened with yoghurt and ground almonds. It is traditionally eaten with bread.

Serves 6

675 g	lamb fillet	1½ lb
	1 onion, chopped	
	1 clove garlic, chopped	
2.5 cm	fresh ginger, peeled and chopped	1 in
	1 green chilli, deseeded and chopped	
	Seeds from 4 green cardamom pods	
30 ml	oil	2 tbsp
5 ml	cinnamon	1 tsp
20 ml	Rogan josh curry powder	4 tsp
30 ml	desiccated (shredded) coconut	2 tbsp
	6 tomatoes, skinned and chopped	
5 ml	salt	1 tsp
45 ml	ground almonds	3 tbsp
150 ml	yoghurt	¼ pt/⅔ cup

1. Wash and dry the lamb and cut into bite-sized pieces.

2. Grind the onion, garlic, ginger, chilli and cardamom seeds to a coarse paste.

3. Fry in the oil in a saucepan until pale gold. Add the lamb and continue to fry briskly for 5 minutes, turning frequently.

4. Stir in the cinnamon, curry powder and coconut and leave over a low heat. Stir in the tomatoes and salt.

5. Bring slowly to the boil, lower the heat and cover. Simmer gently for 1 hour, stirring occasionally.

6. Mix in the almonds and yoghurt and reheat briefly until hot, stirring until the yoghurt is smoothly blended with rest of ingredients.

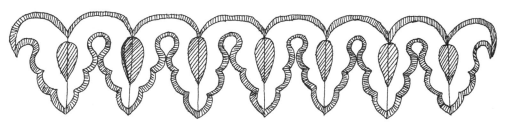

BHINDI GOSHT

LAMB AND OKRA STEW

A subtle grouping of ingredients from the north makes for an appetising contribution which will appeal to all okra enthusiasts. Serve with bread and chutney.

Serves 4

450 g	lamb fillet	1 lb
15 ml	oil	1 tbsp
1 onion, chopped		
1 clove garlic, chopped		
1 cm	fresh ginger, peeled and chopped	½ in
1 green chilli, deseeded and chopped		
175 g	okra	6 oz
2.5 ml	turmeric	½ tsp
1.25 ml	chilli powder	¼ tsp
15 ml	garam masala	1 tbsp
450 ml	water	¾ pt/2 cups
5 ml	salt	1 tsp
150 ml	yoghurt	¼ pt/⅔ cup

1. Wash and dry the lamb and cut into bite-sized pieces. Fry briskly in the oil in a saucepan until meat colour changes from pink to beige.

2. Grind the onion, garlic, ginger and chilli to a fairly coarse paste. Add to the fried lamb and stir well to mix.

3. Top, tail and wash the okra then dry each piece thoroughly. Add to the lamb with all the remaining ingredients except the yoghurt.

4. Slowly bring to the boil then lower the heat and cover. Simmer for 45–60 minutes until the meat is tender, stirring from time to time.

5. Finally mix in the yoghurt and reheat briefly, stirring, until the ingredients are well blended.

GOSHT TIKKA KABABS

MEAT TIKKA KEBABS

*F*ollow the recipe for Murgh Tikka Kababs (page 74), using cubes of lamb fillet instead of chicken.
Serves 4

GOSHT DHANSAK

LAMB DHANSAK

*F*ollow the recipe for Murgh Dhansak (page 96), using cubes of lamb fillet instead of chicken.
Serves 4

GOSHT DO-PIAZA

LAMB DO-PIAZA

*F*ollow the recipe for Murgh Do-piaza (page 94), using cubes of lamb fillet instead of chicken.
Serves 6

GOSHT KORMA

LAMB KORMA

*F*ollow the recipe for Murgh Korma (page 88), using cubes of lamb fillet instead of chicken.
   Serves 4

GOSHT KARI

LAMB CURRY

*M*ake the same sauce as given in the recipe for Sabzi Ka Kari (page 128). Add 675 g/1½ lb diced lean lamb instead of vegetables and simmer, covered, for about 1 hour until meat is tender. Increase salt to taste and stir periodically.
   Serves 6

PHAL GOSHT

PORK PHAL

This is the hottest curry there is, dangerously so, and was invented by the restaurant trade to serve clients keen to see if they could cope with the heat. It's virtually the same as the vindaloo on the next page but with more chilli powder and if you are tempted to try it, beware because it could cause burns to throat and tongue.

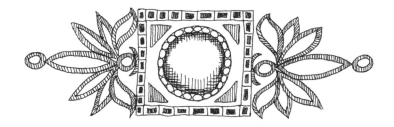

GOSHT VINDALOO

PORK VINDALOO

*F*iery Vindaloo belongs to Goa on the south-west coast, a Portuguese territory until the late 1950s and one of the few places in India where pork is permitted and eaten by the Portuguese Catholics, other Christians in the vicinity and now tourists who have 'discovered' Goa during the last decade and turned it into a stylish holiday resort for Europeans, admired as much for its beauty as for its fine food.

On an historical note, Sharwoods tell us the word Vindaloo is said to come from the Portuguese 'viande e ailio', meaning meat with garlic. Equally important to a Vindaloo is the inclusion of malt vinegar (used in the sub-continent to tenderise meat) and potatoes and it should always be eaten with plenty of rice, hot pickles if you can take it and refreshing yoghurt. If preferred, use beef instead of the pork.

Serves 6

	2 onions, chopped	
	2 cloves garlic, chopped	
2.5 cm	fresh ginger, peeled and chopped	1 in
675 g	pork fillet, diced	1½ lb
45 ml	oil	3 tbsp
	Seeds from 6 green cardamom pods	
10 ml	cinnamon	2 tsp
2.5 ml	ground cloves	½ tsp
5 ml	grated nutmeg OR	1 tsp
15 ml	blades of mace	1 tbsp
15 ml	ground cumin	1 tbsp
20–30 ml	chilli powder	1½–2 tbsp
5 ml	turmeric	1 tsp
45 ml	malt vinegar	3 tbsp
30 ml	tomato purée (paste)	2 tbsp
300 ml	water	½ pt/1¼ cups
7.5 ml	salt	1½ tsp
	2 potatoes	

| **GARNISH:** |
| Salted and coarsely chopped cashew nuts |
| Chopped fresh coriander (cilantro) |

1. Grind the onions, garlic and ginger to a coarse paste.

2. Wash and dry the pork then fry in the oil in a substantial saucepan until the pinky look goes, stirring frequently. Remove to a plate.

3. Add the ground ingredients to the remaining oil in the pan and fry gently until they become pale gold. Mix in all the spices from cardamom to turmeric and continue to fry for a few seconds only.

4. Add the rest of the ingredients except the potatoes. Replace the pork, bring slowly to the boil then cover the pan and simmer gently for 1 hour, stirring occasionally.

5. Meanwhile, peel and wash potatoes and cut into chunks. Add to the pan and continue to simmer, covered, for a further 20 minutes. Stir 3–4 times.

6. Transfer to warm plates and sprinkle each portion with the cashews and coriander.

SORPOTEL

MEAT AND LIVER STEW

 strong and powerful Goan stew which is a close relative of the vindaloo. Watch out for the heat of the chillies.
Serves 6

450 g	pork fillet, diced	1 lb
5 ml	turmeric	1 tsp
7.5 ml	salt	1½ tsp
300 ml	water	½ pt/1¼ cups
	4 onions, chopped	
	4 cloves garlic, chopped	
2.5 cm	fresh ginger, peeled and chopped	1 in
	2-6 dried red chillies, deseeded and chopped	
30 ml	oil	2 tbsp
15 ml	ground cumin	1 tbsp
15 ml	garam masala	1 tbsp
	Pinch of ground clove	
350 g	pig's or lamb's liver, diced	12 oz
60 ml	vinegar	4 tbsp
	Extra salt	

1. Put the pork into a saucepan with the turmeric, salt and water. Bring to the boil then simmer, covered, for 40 minutes.

2. Meanwhile, grind the onions, garlic, ginger and chillies to a coarse paste. Fry in the oil in a separate pan until golden. Mix in the spices and leave over a low heat. Add the liver and fry for 10 minutes over medium heat, turning from time to time.

3. Drain the pork and mix into the fried liver and spices. Leave uncovered and fry for a further 10 minutes, stirring. Mix in the vinegar and enough of the pork liquid to make a thick sauce. Season with extra salt to taste. Reheat and serve very hot with rice and dhal.

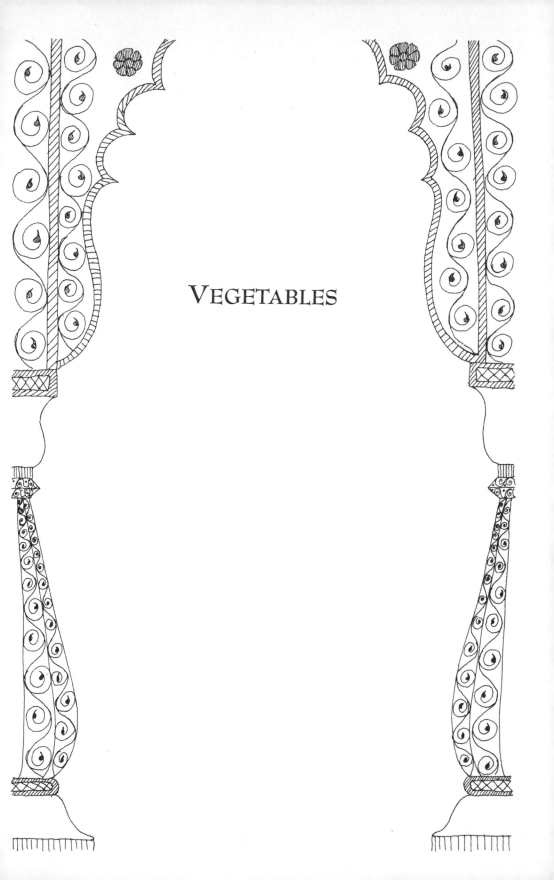

VEGETABLES

CHANNA MASALA

SAVOURY CHICK PEAS

A *short-cut spicy pulse dish. In northern India where this originates, it is always eaten with fried bread called bhatura, but warmed-up croissants taste equally good.*

Serves 4

1 onion, chopped		
1 clove garlic, chopped		
2.5 cm	fresh ginger, peeled and chopped	1 in
2 green chillies, deseeded and chopped		
2.5ml	cumin seeds	½ tsp
15 ml	oil	1 tbsp
5 ml	garam masala	1 tsp
1.5 ml	cinnamon	¼ tsp
425 g	canned undrained chick peas (garbanzos)	about 15 oz/ 2 cups
2.5 ml	turmeric	½ tsp
15 ml	tomato purée (paste)	1 tbsp
15 ml	lemon juice	1 tbsp

1. Grind the onion, garlic, ginger, chillies and cumin seeds to a coarse paste. Fry in the oil in a saucepan until pale gold then mix in all the remaining ingredients.

2. Heat through, uncovered, for 5 minutes, stirring. Serve very hot.

Rajma Masala

SAVOURY RED KIDNEY BEANS

*M*ake as opposite, substituting a can of red kidney beans for the chick peas.

Serves 4

SABZI KA KARI

VEGETABLE CURRY

A medium hot Anglo-Indian vegetable curry in an appetising, full-flavoured and versatile sauce which can also be used for making basic curries of meat, poultry, fish and eggs. To save time, you can double up on all the sauce ingredients and freeze half for later use. Serve the curry with rice, chutney and any of the side dishes given in the accompaniments section.

Serves 6

	SAUCE:	
30 ml	oil	2 tbsp
10 ml	black mustard seeds	2 tsp
	2 large onions, chopped	
	2 cloves garlic, chopped	
2.5 cm	fresh ginger, peeled and chopped	1 in
	2 green chillies, deseeded and chopped	
5 ml	turmeric	1 tsp
10 ml	EACH ground cumin, ground coriander (cilantro) and mild Korma curry powder	2 tsp
2.5 ml	chilli powder (or more to taste)	½ tsp
1.5 ml	fenugreek	¼ tsp
30 ml	tomato purée (paste)	2 tbsp
45 ml	hot water	3 tbsp
	1 large bay leaf	
	2 dried curry leaves, crumbled (optional)	
2.5 cm	cinnamon stick	1 in
10 ml	salt	2 tsp
	5 tomatoes, skinned and chopped	
250 ml	warm water	8 fl oz/1 cup
45 ml	chopped fresh coriander (cilantro)	3 tbsp

VEGETABLE SELECTION:
1 small head of broccoli
½ medium head of cauliflower
1 aubergine (eggplant), diced
2 courgettes (zucchini), thinly sliced
225 g fresh green beans, cut into chunks   8 oz

TO FINISH:		
45 ml	instant coconut milk powder	3 tbsp
75 ml	warm water	5 tbsp

1. Heat the oil in a large saucepan. Add the mustard seeds and two-thirds cover the pan with a lid. Fry over a low heat for a few seconds until they stop spluttering. Take the pan off the heat.

2. Grind the onions, garlic, ginger and chillies to a coarse paste. Add to the saucepan and stand the pan over a medium heat. Fry until pale gold, stirring.

3. Work in all the spices from the turmeric to the fenugreek then splash in some cold water to stop the spices from burning.

4. Combine the tomato purée with the hot water and add to pan with all remaining ingredients except the vegetables. Simmer, covered, for 45 minutes, stirring occasionally.

5. Meanwhile, wash the vegetables and break the broccoli and cauliflower into small florets.

6. Add all the vegetables to the pan of sauce, bring to the boil, lower the heat and cover. Simmer for 20–25 minutes or until tender. Remove bay leaf.

7. Finally mix in the coconut powder smoothly blended with water. Reheat briefly.

BHARI SIMLA MIRICH

STUFFED MIXED PEPPERS

V isually vibrant and economical to make, these filled peppers from the Punjab are a vegetarian meal in themselves and are also companionable with drier curries of meat and poultry.
Serves 4

PEPPERS:		
4 large mixed colour (bell) peppers: green, yellow, orange and red		
4 large cooked potatoes, diced		
1 onion, chopped		
3 bottled pickled peppers, each about 10 cm/4 in in length, squeezed dry and finely chopped		
30 ml	oil	2 tbsp
5 ml	salt	1 tsp

SAUCE:		
1 onion, chopped		
2.5 cm	fresh ginger, peeled and chopped	1 in
2 green chillies, deseeded and chopped		
15 ml	oil	1 tbsp
400 g	canned tomatoes in tomato juice	14 oz
1 dried red chilli (optional)		
10 ml	Korma curry powder	2 tsp
5 ml	salt	1 tsp
150 ml	water	¼ pt/⅔ cup

1. Wash the peppers, cut off the tops and leave on one side for the time being. Remove the inside fibres and seeds from each.

2. Fry the potatoes, onion and pickled peppers in the oil in a saucepan for about 5–6 minutes or until pale golden brown. Stir in the salt.

3. Spoon the filling into the peppers and stand upright and close together in a saucepan.

4. To make the sauce, grind the onion, ginger and chillies to a paste. Fry in the oil in a saucepan until light golden brown.

5. Mash the tomatoes in their juice and add to the onion mixture with the red chilli (if using), curry powder, salt and water. Bring to the boil, stirring. Then simmer for 5 minutes.

6. Spoon round the peppers. Cover the saucepan with a lid and simmer gently for 1 hour. Serve hot or cold.

AVIYAL

MIXED VEGETABLES IN CURRY SAUCE

n elegant and delicate vegetable mix from Kerala in the south which is slightly piquant and subtly spiced, this can be eaten on its own with rice and a sharp pickle or chutney, or take its place as part of a vegetarian buffet. The canned coconut milk makes the sauce seem much richer than it actually is, a bonus for slimmers.

Serves 6

675 g	mixed vegetables, choosing a	1½ lb
	selection from:	
	fresh or frozen sliced beans	
	peeled and chopped onions	
	diced aubergine (eggplant)	
	squares of red and green (bell) peppers	
	broccoli and cauliflower florets	
	diced potatoes	
	peeled carrot slices	

	SAUCE:	
	2 cloves garlic, chopped	
2.5 cm	fresh ginger, peeled and chopped	1 in
10 ml	cumin seeds	2 tsp
30 ml	oil	2 tbsp
5 ml	turmeric	1 tsp
400 ml	canned coconut milk	14 fl oz/1¾ cups
	Juice of 1 lime or lemon	
7.5 ml	salt	1½ tsp
150 ml	yoghurt	¼ pt/⅔ cup

1. Thoroughly wash the vegetables and leave on one side for the time being.

2. To make the sauce, grind the garlic, ginger and cumin seeds to a paste.

3. Heat the oil in a pan. Add the garlic mixture and turmeric then fry over a medium heat for about 3 minutes. If necessary, splash in a little cold water to stop ingredients from burning.

4. Add all the remaining sauce ingredients followed by the vegetables. Slowly bring to the boil, stirring. Cover and simmer for 10 minutes.

5. Uncover and continue to simmer for 20 minutes, stirring frequently. Serve very hot.

MASALA BHINDI

CURRIED OKRA

n okra speciality from the north which can be eaten by itself as a vegetarian main course with bread, or served to accompany meat and poultry main courses. It has a warm orange colour and is slightly hot.

Serves 6

450 g	okra (ladies' fingers)	1 lb
	1 onion, chopped	
	1 clove garlic, chopped	
1 cm	fresh ginger, peeled and chopped	½ in
	1 green chilli, deseeded and chopped	
30 ml	oil	2 tbsp
	4 tomatoes, skinned and chopped	
5 ml	medium hot Bombay curry powder	1 tsp
150 ml	water	¼ pt/⅔ cup
15 ml	tomato purée (paste)	1 tbsp
2.5 ml	salt	½ tsp
30 ml	chopped fresh coriander (cilantro)	2 tbsp

1. Top and tail the okra then wash and dry each one individually to stop it from becoming sticky.

2. Grind the onion, garlic, ginger and chilli to a coarse paste.

3. Fry in the oil in a saucepan until light golden brown. Add all remaining ingredients including okra. Bring to the boil, stirring. Lower the heat and cover.

4. Simmer for 15-20 minutes or until the okra is tender, stirring twice.

ALOO BOMBAY

BOMBAY POTATOES

useful and tasty side dish from the west which goes well with all kinds of meat, poultry and vegetable curries. It is dry, like ordinary fried potatoes, so don't expect a sauce.

Serves 4–5

30 ml	oil	2 tbsp
5 ml	black mustard seeds	1 tsp
	1 onion, sliced into rings	
2.5 ml	turmeric	½ tsp
5 ml	garam masala	1 tsp
1.5 ml	chilli powder	¼ tsp
1.5 ml	fenugreek	¼ tsp
7.5 ml	Bombay curry powder	1½ tsp
450–500 g	cooked potatoes	1 lb

1. Heat the oil in a saucepan, add the mustard seeds, two-thirds cover the pan with a lid and fry for 30–40 seconds or until the seeds stop spluttering.

2. Add the onion rings and fry gently until golden. Mix in all the spices and curry powder. Fry briefly over a low heat.

3. Cut the potatoes into small cubes. Add to the pan and reheat until golden brown, stirring often so that they colour evenly and look uniform. Serve hot.

ALOO METHI

FRIED POTATOES WITH FRESH FENUGREEK

ot unlike spinach in taste, fresh fenugreek leaves are watercress-sized or maybe a little bigger and have an elusively mild flavour. You will need to go to an Indian area to find them and they need thorough washing.

Serves 4

To make, follow the recipe for Aloo Bombay, adding about 50 g/2 oz/1 cup loosely packed fenugreek leaves with the potatoes and fry together for same length of time.

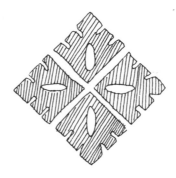

ALOO SAG

POTATOES WITH SPINACH

his recipe is adapted from a north Indian one given to me by Chef Rohinton Ankelsaria of the vegetarian Diwana restaurant in London's Euston. It has a bit of heat to it so omit the chillies if you can't take it.

Serves 6

150 g loosely packed spinach leaves 5 oz/10 cups		
1 large onion, chopped		
1 clove garlic, chopped		
2.5 cm	fresh ginger, peeled and chopped	1 in
30 ml	oil	2 tbsp
5 ml	turmeric	1 tsp
15 ml	garam masala	1 tbsp
2 dried red chillies (optional)		
550 g	cooked and diced potatoes	1¼ lb
100 ml	water	3½ fl oz/6½ tbsp
5 ml	salt	1 tsp

1. Wash and dry the spinach and chop finely.

2. Grind the onion, garlic and ginger to a coarse paste. Fry in the oil in a saucepan until light gold then stir in the turmeric, garam masala and chillies, if used.

3. Mix in the chopped spinach, potatoes, water and salt. Bring slowly to the boil, lower the heat and cover.

4. Simmer for about 7 minutes, stirring a few times. Uncover and continue to cook over a minimal heat until most of the liquid has evaporated. Stir often to prevent sticking.

ALOO GOBI

POTATOES AND CAULIFLOWER

nother northern classic and a successful partnership of
ingredients.
Serves 6

*Follow the recipe for the Aloo Sag (page 137) above but use the florets of
1 small cauliflower instead of the spinach. Also increase water to
300 ml/½ pt/1¼ cups. A little extra salt may be needed, depending on
personal taste.*

VEGETARIAN MAIN COURSES

IDLIS

RICE CAKES

*S*now-white rice cakes, made from a type of pulse called urad dhal, are always starred on Indian vegetarian menus as something too good to miss. With coconut chutney and raitas, they are a special feast, original, a culinary experience from the mostly vegetarian south. If you wonder why idlis tend to be more expensive in restaurants than other main courses, it is because they are labour-intensive to make and literally cooked while you wait. Unless you want to spend extra money on kitchen utensils, the thing to use at home is an egg poacher with four indentations.

Serves 4

100 g	white urad dhal	4 oz/about 1 cup
225 g	Basmati rice	8 oz/1 cup
300 ml	cold water	½ pt/1¼ cups
5 ml	salt	1 tsp
1.5 ml	baking powder	¼ tsp

1. Wash the dhal and rice in several changes of cold water.

2. Tip into a large bowl, add plenty of cold water, cover and leave to soak for 8–12 hours. Drain.

3. Grind the dhal, rice and cold water together in a heavy-duty blender or food processor until it looks like lightly whipped thick cream.

4. Spoon into a clean bowl, mix in the salt and cover. Leave in a warm place to ferment overnight or a minimum of 8 hours. The linen cupboard is as good a place as any.

5. Before cooking, stir round with the baking powder and ensure the mixture is smooth.

6. Well-grease egg poacher cups, two-thirds fill with the idli mixture, cover and poach for 10 minutes when the cakes should have risen and look cooked through and white.

7. Turn out on to a warm plate and keep hot by standing over a pan of gently simmering water. Repeat, using up the rest of mixture to make 16–18 cakes. Serve straight away.

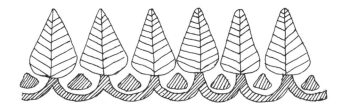

DOSA

PANCAKES

D osa are THE ultimate pancake of the East, vast by our standards and one of the most substantial meals you could ever have. Chefs fold them with immaculate expertise into long tubes, fans and cones but the ordinary Indian housewife tucks in filling and folds them in half – straightforward but still marvellous if you like classy simplicity. Mine are a copy of ones I have eaten in Indian homes, delicious but please be warned: they do require patience to put together so allow plenty of time for trial and error. Allow one pancake per person.

Makes about 6

	POTATO FILLING:	
	1 onion, chopped	
	1 green chilli, deseeded and chopped	
15 ml	oil	1 tbsp
5 ml	black mustard seeds	1 tsp
5 ml	Korma curry powder (mild)	1 tsp
2.5 ml	ground coriander (cilantro)	½ tsp
10 ml	turmeric	2 tsp
450 g	freshly cooked potatoes, water reserved	1 lb
5 ml	salt	1 tsp

	PANCAKE MIXTURE:	
225 g	basmati rice	8 oz/1 cup
100 g	white urad dhal	4 oz/about 1 cup
5 ml	whole fenugreek	1 tsp
300 ml	warm water	½ pt/1¼ cups
30 ml	besan or gram flour	2 tbsp
75 ml	cold water	5 tbsp

1. Make the filling first then leave, covered, in the refrigerator until ready to complete the pancakes.

2. Grind the onion and chilli to a paste.

3. Pour the oil into a pan. Add mustard seeds, two-thirds cover the pan with a lid and fry for about 10 seconds until seeds have stopped popping. Add the onion and chilli.

4. Stir in the curry powder, coriander and turmeric and remove from the heat temporarily.

5. Drain the potatoes, reserving 150 ml/¼ pt/⅔ cup of cooking water. Cut the potatoes into fairly small cubes and add to the pan of spices with the reserved cooking water and salt.

6. Bring to the boil, lower the heat and cover. Simmer for about 10 minutes or until the potatoes are soft but still moist. Cool, cover and refrigerate.

7. To make the pancakes, wash the rice and dhal in several changes of cold water. Tip into a bowl, add plenty of cold water, cover and leave to soak for 12 hours.

8. Drain. Transfer the rice and dhal to a heavy-duty blender or food processor, add the fenugreek and warm water and grind to a thick, creamy and smooth batter.

9. Return to a clean bowl, cover and leave to ferment in a warm place, such as a linen cupboard, for 8–10 hours.

10. Sift in the besan flour, which deepens the colour of the batter, then gradually and lightly beat in the cold water.

11. Brush a large, 23 cm/9 in frying pan, preferably non-stick, with oil. Add 45 ml/3 tbsp of the pancake batter and spread from the centre outwards to cover the base of the pan. The best thing to use here is the back of a tablespoon.

12. Cover with a plate or lid and fry for 3 minutes. Carefully turn over with two spatulas and fry, covered, for another 2 minutes.

13. Turn out on to a work top lined with foil, add equal amounts of reheated filling to each and fold over to form semi-circles. Eat straight away with coconut chutney and Tarka Dhal (page 158).

SAMBHAR

CURRIED LENTILS AND VEGETABLES

southern speciality which can be eaten as a main meal or appetiser with rice. Choose the vegetables from diced potatoes, cauliflower or broccoli florets, skinned and chopped tomatoes, cubed marrow or pumpkin, chopped pepper, sliced carrots or sliced beans.
Serves 4–6

	1 large onion, chopped	
	1 clove garlic, chopped	
1 cm	fresh ginger, peeled and chopped	½ in
	1 green chilli, deseeded and chopped	
15 ml	oil	1 tbsp
225 g	orange lentils	8 oz/1 cup
750 ml	boiling water	1¼ pt/3 cups
45 ml	lemon juice	3 tbsp
2.5 ml	turmeric	½ tsp
10 ml	medium Bombay curry powder	2 tsp
7.5 ml	salt	1½ tsp
450 g	cooked mixed vegetables	1 lb

	SPICY OIL (TARKA):	
30 ml	oil	2 tbsp
5 ml	cumin seeds	1 tsp
5 ml	black mustard seeds	1 tsp

GARNISH:
Fried onion rings
Chopped fresh coriander (cilantro)

1. Grind the onion, garlic, ginger and chilli to a paste. Fry in the oil in a saucepan until light gold.

2. Stir in the lentils, water, lemon juice, turmeric, curry powder and salt. Bring to the boil, lower the heat and cover. Simmer for 15 minutes, stirring frequently.

3. Uncover and continue to simmer for 10 minutes, stirring often. Stir in the vegetables.

4. Just before the vegetables are cooked, make the spicy oil. Heat the oil in a small saucepan until just sizzling. Add the seeds, two-thirds cover the pan with a lid and continue to cook until they stop popping.

5. Spoon the dhal into a warm serving dish and trickle the hot savoury oil over the top. Garnish with the onion rings and coriander.

MATAR PANEER

INDIAN CHEESE WITH MINT AND TOMATOES

A *top-class vegetarian dish from the Punjab with warmth and colour, light but sustaining, quite delicious with bread and a yoghurt raita at any time of year. If you don't want to make your own paneer, which is the main ingredient, look for it in an Indian shop or substitute unsmoked tofu which is readily available everywhere.*

Serves 4–6

225 g	Paneer (see page 150) or tofu	8 oz
	1 egg white, lightly beaten	
	Flour	
45 ml	oil	3 tbsp
	1 clove garlic, chopped	
2.5 cm	fresh ginger, peeled and chopped	1 in
5 ml	EACH black mustard seeds, turmeric, ground coriander (cilantro), ground cumin and paprika	1 tsp
10 ml	garam masala	2 tsp
10 ml	chopped fresh mint	2 tsp
400 g	tomatoes, skinned and chopped	14 oz
10 ml	tomato purée (paste)	2 tsp
7.5 ml	salt	1½ tsp
175 g	frozen peas	6 oz/1½ cups
150 ml	thick yoghurt	¼ pt/⅔ cup

1. Cut the paneer or well-drained tofu into 2.5 cm/1 in cubes and coat liberally with beaten egg white followed by flour.

2. Fry fairly briskly in the oil in a frying pan until light golden brown. Drain on crumpled kitchen paper. Take the pan off the heat.

3. Grind the garlic and ginger to a paste. Add to the pan of oil with all the spices from mustard seeds to garam masala.

4. Two-thirds cover with a lid and heat for a few seconds until the mustard seeds stop popping. Splash in a little cold water to prevent the spices from burning.

5. Add the mint, tomatoes, tomato purée, salt, peas and paneer or tofu.

6. Slowly bring to the boil and cover. Simmer gently for 10 minutes then stir in the yoghurt and heat through for 5 minutes before serving.

PALAK PANEER SAK

INDIAN CHEESE WITH SPINACH AND CREAM

 tasty and much favoured vegetarian speciality from the north with a memorable taste, this is good with warm bread.
Serves 4–5

225 g	Paneer (see page 150) or tofu	8 oz
	1 egg white, lightly beaten	
	Flour	
45 ml	oil	3 tbsp
5 ml	EACH white mustard seeds,	1 tsp
fenugreek seeds, ground cumin, ground ginger,		
garam masala and ground coriander (cilantro)		
5 ml	salt	1 tsp
	1 clove garlic, crushed	
400 g	canned, chopped spinach	14 oz/1¾ cups
75 ml	tomato purée (paste)	5 tbsp
10 ml	sugar	2 tsp
60 ml	single (light) cream	4 tbsp
20 ml	chopped fresh coriander (cilantro)	4 tsp

1. Drain the paneer or tofu if necessary and cut into 1 cm/½ in cubes. Coat liberally in the egg white, followed by flour.

2. Heat the oil in a non-stick and capacious frying pan. Add the paneer or tofu cubes and fry until light golden brown. Remove from the pan and drain on crumpled kitchen paper.

3. To the remaining oil in the pan, add all the spices from the mustard seeds to ground coriander with the salt and garlic. Stir-fry for 2 minutes over a low heat, adding a splash of cold water to prevent the spices from burning.

4. Mix in all remaining ingredients except the fresh coriander, replace the paneer or tofu and heat through gently for 6 minutes, stirring gently from time to time.

5. To serve, spoon into a warm dish and sprinkle with the fresh coriander.

PANEER

INDIAN CHEESE

A concentrated and firm cheese, white in colour and bland, which closely resembles tofu, this is a national dish which can often be found in Indian supermarkets.

Makes 550 g/1¼ lb

3.5 l	full cream milk	6 pt/15 cups
60 ml	malt vinegar	4 tbsp

1. Bring the milk to the boil in a large pan, stirring continuously.

2. With the pan still over a low heat, add the vinegar. Continue to cook until the milk breaks up and forms fairly solid curds in a liquidy whey.

3. Tip carefully into a colander lined with a large piece of muslin then lift up the edges of the cloth so that the whey can drain away.

4. As soon as only curds remain, rinse them under cold running water to remove the vinegary taste.

5. Twist the muslin tightly round the curds, tie up with string and hang the parcel over a sink or bowl until all the dripping has stopped. The paneer is now ready for use.

BIRIYANIS

MURGH BIRIYANI

CHICKEN BIRIYANI

*I*t could be said that there is a tenuous connection between India's biriyani and Spain's paella, perhaps reflecting centuries of East-West ties brought about by exploration and trade. Both look similar, are brightly coloured, decoratively garnished, mild to the taste, dry, rice-based, flavoured with saffron and enhanced with meat or fish or poultry. A feast!
Serves 8

1 kg	boned chicken breasts	2 lb
	MARINADE:	
	2 onions, chopped	
	2 cloves garlic, chopped	
2.5 cm	fresh ginger, peeled and chopped	1 in
	2 green chillies, deseeded and chopped	
	Seeds from 5 green cardamom pods	
2.5 cm	cinnamon stick	1 in
10 ml	blades of mace	2 tsp
15 ml	light poppy seeds	1 tbsp
	6 fresh mint leaves	
450 ml	thick yoghurt	¾ pt/2 cups
7.5 ml	salt	1½ tsp
	FOR FRYING:	
	1 large onion, finely chopped	
30 ml	oil	2 tbsp
	RICE:	
5 ml	saffron strands	1 tsp
15 ml	boiling water	1 tbsp
450 g	basmati rice	1 lb/2 cups
10 ml	salt	2 tsp
	Water for cooking	
30 ml	butter or ghee, melted	2 tbsp

GARNISH:		
Thin slices of fried onions		
60 ml	almond flakes, toasted	4 tbsp
15 ml	raisins	1 tbsp
3 hard-boiled (hard-cooked) eggs, shelled and sliced		

1. Wash, dry and skin the chicken then cut the flesh into smallish cubes.

2. Make the marinade. Grind the onions, garlic, ginger, chillies, cardamom seeds and cinnamon stick to a paste. Transfer to a fairly large dish.

3. Work in the mace, poppy seeds, torn-up mint leaves, yoghurt and salt. Add the chicken and toss over and over in the marinade until each piece is well coated. Cover and refrigerate for 2 hours.

4. Fry the onion in the oil in a roomy saucepan until it turns pale gold. Stir in the chicken cubes plus the marinade.

5. Bring to the boil, lower the heat and cover. Simmer gently for 30 minutes. Uncover and continue to cook until about half the liquid has evaporated. Stir frequently. Keep hot.

6. About 20 minutes before the chicken is ready, soak the saffron in the boiling water for 10 minutes. Add to the rice (already in a pan) with the salt and water and follow the pack directions for method of cooking and time to allow.

7. Put half the cooked rice into a casserole and cover completely with the chicken mixture. Spread rest of rice on top and moisten with the melted butter or ghee.

8. Garnish tastefully with the fried onions, almonds, raisins and shelled eggs. Serve straight away.

GOSHT BIRIYANI

BIRIYANI WITH LAMB

Prepare as the Murgh Biriyani (page 152), using cubed fillet of lamb instead of the chicken.

JINGA BIRIYANI

BIRIYANI WITH PRAWNS

Prepare as the Murgh Biriyani (page 152), using peeled prawns instead of the chicken. Cook fish for 5 minutes only.

KHUMB BIRIYANI

BIRIYANI WITH MUSHROOMS

Prepare as the Murgh Biriyani (page 152), using 1 kg/2 lb sliced mushrooms (mixed varieties, according to taste) instead of the chicken. Marinate for 1 hour only and reduce the cooking time to 5 minutes.

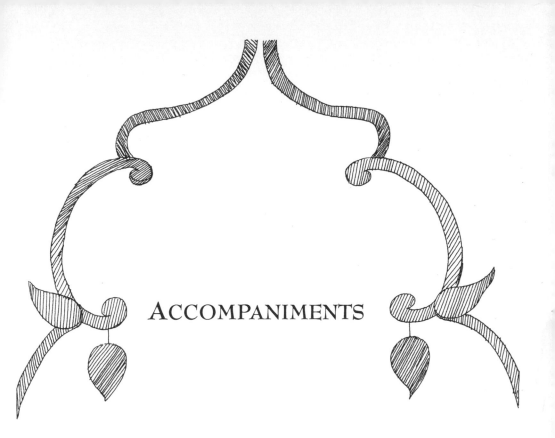

ACCOMPANIMENTS

CHAWAL

RICE

*R*ice is the staple food everywhere in India except in the north where bread takes over. Basmati, grown in the foothills of the Himalayas, is the best there is for top quality Indian cooking and with its fine and elegant grains, is guaranteed to stay firm, dry and unbroken.

To cook rice:

As there are so many brands now on the market, follow pack directions EXACTLY, as I have found they vary from one brand to another. Leave the cooked rice plain or gently fork in a little butter, margarine or ghee.

CHAWAL PILAU

SAVOURY RICE

*C*ook rice as directed on the packet or bag, using stock instead of water. Colour by adding a little turmeric at the beginning of cooking and flavour with a few cardamom seeds taken from 2–3 pods, 5 ml/1 tsp garam masala, 2 cloves and 2 skinned and chopped tomatoes. Gently fork in a little butter, margarine or ghee just before serving. Garnish with fried onion rings, wedges of hard-boiled (hardcooked) egg and tomatoes and sprays of fresh coriander (cilantro). If preferred, leave plain.

CHAWAL SAFFRAN

SAFFRON RICE

Soak 2.5 ml/½ tsp of saffron strands for 30 minutes in 15 ml/1 tbsp of boiling water. Add to the cooking liquid.

RED AND YELLOW RICE

You will often see this in Indian restaurants and in the home and it is characteristic of the Indians' love of colour.

Use plain boiled rice or savoury rice for this. As soon as it is cooked, divide into 2 equal portions. Sprinkle one portion with a sparing amount of red food colour, the other with a few shakes of turmeric. Fork both together, transfer to a heatproof dish, cover and reheat in a warm oven. You will get a lovely speckled red and yellow effect which is almost symbolic of India's most widely grown flower – the marigold.

TARKA DHAL

SPICY LENTILS

A meal accompaniment for vegetarian and non-vegetarian specialities alike, the dhal is an appetising pulse dish which, when eaten solo with rice, is nutritionally sound. No additional protein is necessary. It comes from the north.

Serves 6

	1 large onion, chopped	
	1 clove garlic, chopped	
1 cm	fresh ginger, peeled and chopped	½ in
	1 green chilli, deseeded and chopped	
15 ml	oil	1 tbsp
225 g	orange lentils	8 oz/1⅓ cups
750 ml	boiling water	1¼ pts/3 cups
2.5 ml	turmeric	½ tsp
7.5 ml	salt	1½ tsp

	SPICY OIL (TARKA):	
30 ml	oil	2 tbsp
5 ml	cumin seeds	1 tsp
5 ml	black mustard seeds	1 tsp

1. Grind the onion, garlic, ginger and chilli to a paste. Fry in the oil in a saucepan until light gold.

2. Stir in the lentils, water, turmeric and salt. Bring to the boil, lower the heat and cover. Simmer for 15 minutes, stirring frequently.

3. Uncover and continue to simmer for 10 minutes, stirring often.

4. Just before the lentils are cooked, make the spicy oil. Heat the oil in a small saucepan until just sizzling. Add the seeds, two-thirds cover the pan with a lid and continue to cook until they stop popping.

5. Spoon the dhal into a warm serving dish and trickle the hot savoury oil over the top.

KARI DHAL

CURRIED DHAL

M̶ake exactly as above but increase the heat in the dish by adding an extra chilli. Also include a bay leaf and 2 curry leaves if available.

KITCHERIE

RICE AND GREEN LENTILS

 soft and gentle dhal and rice mixture from the south which makes a perfect foil for local hot curries such as the vindaloo. Serves 6–8

225 g	green lentils, no-soak variety	8 oz/1⅓ cups
450 g	basmati rice	1 lb/2½ cups
	1 large onion, chopped	
30 ml	oil	2 tbsp
1.25 l	cold water	2¼ pts/5⅝ cups
15 ml	salt	1 tbsp
	6 green cardamom pods	
	4 cloves	

1. Whatever the packet says, soak the lentils for 2 hours in cold water or they will remain hard after the rice is cooked. Wash the rice separately and leave on one side temporarily.

2. Fry the onion in the oil in a roomy saucepan until light golden brown. Drain the lentils and add to the pan, together with the washed rice.

3. Mix in all the remaining ingredients then bring to the boil, stirring continuously.

4. Lower the heat and cover. Simmer for about 15 minutes when both the lentils and rice should be cooked, stirring frequently.

TAMATTAR BHURTA

TOMATO CHUTNEY

*ne of the most cooling side dishes imaginable, scented with lime
and ginger and adapted from a recipe put out many years ago
by a Government department dealing with the cooking of ethnic groups.
It is the most flavoursome uncooked chutney there is and marvellous
with hot curries. Imagine eating snowflakes! It comes from southern
India.*

Serves about 8

	8 tomatoes	
	1 small onion, chopped	
1 cm	fresh ginger, peeled and chopped	½ in
	1 green chilli, deseeded and chopped	
7.5 cm	strip of lime peel, chopped	3 in
5 ml	paprika	1 tsp
2.5 ml	turmeric	½ tsp
2.5 ml	salt	½ tsp
1.5 ml	ground coriander (cilantro)	¼ tsp

1. Blanch, skin and chop tomatoes then tip into a bowl.

2. Grind the onion, ginger, chilli and lime peel to a paste.

3. Gradually mix into the tomatoes with remaining
ingredients. Cover and chill up to 5 days in the refrigerator.

RAITAS

YOGHURT SIDE DISHES

group name for the light, refreshing and healthy yoghurt-based condiments served nationally with Indian main courses, especially the hot vegetarian ones from the south. Always use thick yoghurt such as sheep's milk from Greece because it most resembles Indian varieties, often made from buffalo milk and as thick as rich cream cheese.

ALOO RAITA

POTATO RAITA

Serves 4

150 g	thick yoghurt	¼ pt/⅔ cup
	1 small onion, chopped	
	1 green chilli, deseeded and chopped	
	2 cooked and peeled potatoes, diced	
	1-2 pinches of chilli powder	
	2 pinches of ground cumin	
	Salt	
	Chopped fresh coriander (cilantro) or mint	

1. Tip the yoghurt into a bowl.

2. Add the onion, chilli and potatoes.

3. Season with the chilli powder, cumin and salt to taste. Stir well to mix. Transfer to a small bowl and sprinkle with the coriander or mint. Chill lightly before serving.

GAJAR RAITA

CARROT RAITA

ake as the Aloo Raita, substituting 2 medium peeled and finely grated raw carrots for the potatoes. Add 10 ml/2 tsp finely chopped fresh mint with the spices. Chill lightly before serving.
Serves 4

PODEENA RAITA

MINT RAITA

Serves 4

2.5 ml	black mustard seeds	½ tsp
2.5 ml	cumin seeds	½ tsp
10 ml	oil	2 tsp
15 g	fresh mint leaves, loosely packed	½ oz/1 cup
150 ml	thick yoghurt	¼ pt/⅔ cup
	Salt	
	Chilli powder	

1. Put the mustard and cumin seeds into a small pan with the oil. Two-thirds cover with a lid and fry gently until the seeds stop spluttering.

2. Remove the pan from heat. Wash mint and chop finely. Stir into the yoghurt with the fried seeds and any leftover oil.

3. Season to taste with salt, spoon into a small bowl and sprinkle lightly with chilli powder. Chill before serving.

KHEERA RAITA

CUCUMBER RAITA

Serves 4

	½ medium cucumber	
1 cm	fresh ginger, peeled and chopped	½ in
	1 green chilli, deseeded and chopped	
150 ml	thick yoghurt	¼ pt/⅔ cup
2.5 ml	ground cumin	½ tsp
	Salt	

1. Wash and dry the cucumber then grate coarsely. Wring as dry as possible in a tea towel.

2. Grind the ginger and chilli to a paste. Stir into the yoghurt with the cumin and cucumber then season to taste with salt.

3. Transfer to a small bowl and chill lightly before serving.

KEELA RAITA

BANANA RAITA

Serves 4

	1 banana	
150 ml	thick yoghurt	¼ pt/⅔ cup
10 ml	lemon juice	2 tsp
1.5 ml	ground cumin	¼ tsp
1.5 ml	ground cardamom	¼ tsp
10 ml	sugar	2 tsp
	Pinch of salt	

1. Thinly slice the banana into a bowl.

2. Add all remaining ingredients, mix well and cover. Chill lightly before serving.

BRINJAL RAITA

AUBERGINE RAITA

Serves 4

	1 aubergine (eggplant)	
	1 green chilli, deseeded and finely chopped	
15 ml	oil	1 tbsp
150 ml	thick yoghurt	¼ pt/⅔ cup
2.5 ml	ground fenugreek	½ tsp
2.5 ml	ground cumin	½ tsp
5 ml	salt	1 tsp

1. Wash and dry the aubergine and cut into slender chips without removing the skin.

2. Fry the aubergine and chilli in the oil in a pan for 7 minutes, keeping covered. Remove from the heat.

3. Stir into the yoghurt with the remaining ingredients. Cover and chill lightly.

PUDINA CHUTNEY

MINT CHUTNEY

A fresh and refreshing bright green chutney side dish from Assam, this is especially recommended for Shami Kababs and Shahi Kababs on pages 110 and 111. Despite the large amounts of seemingly strong ingredients, the chutney is surprisingly mild and delicately cooling. Stored airtight in a plastic container, it will keep for up to 2 weeks in the refrigerator in winter, about half that in summer.

Serves 8–10

75 g mint leaves, loosely packed 3 oz/about 6 cups		
1 onion, chopped		
2.5 cm fresh ginger, peeled and chopped		1 in
2 cloves garlic, chopped		
2 green chillies, deseeded and chopped		
60 ml	fresh strained lemon juice	4 tbsp
5 ml	sugar	1 tsp
5 ml	salt	1 tsp

1. Rinse the mint and put into a food processor with water still clinging to the leaves.

2. Add the onion, ginger, garlic, chillies, lemon juice, sugar and salt. Process until fairly smooth.

3. Transfer to an airtight container and refrigerate up to 1 week.

DAHNIA CHUTNEY

CORIANDER CHUTNEY

Make exactly as Pudina Chutney, using fresh coriander (cilantro) instead of the mint.
Serves 8–10

NARIYAL CHUTNEY

COCONUT CHUTNEY

Widely eaten in southern India with vegetarian meals, this makes an unusual accompaniment and is speckled a pretty green colour from the coriander. It can be as hot or as mild as you please, depending on the number of green chillies included.
Serves 6–8

150 g	desiccated (shredded) coconut	5 oz/1⅔ cups
300 ml	boiling water	½ pt/1¼ cups
30 ml	finely chopped fresh coriander (cilantro)	2 tbsp
2 green chillies (or more to taste), deseeded and chopped		
1 cm	fresh ginger, peeled and chopped	½ in
5 ml	salt	1 tsp
2 large pinches of chilli powder		
10 ml	oil	2 tsp
5 ml	black mustard seeds	1 tsp

1. In a basin, combine the coconut and water then stir in the coriander.

2. Grind the chillies and ginger to a paste then add to the coconut with the salt and chilli powder.

3. Heat the oil in a small pan, add the mustard seeds and two-thirds cover with a lid. Fry until the seeds stop popping then stir into the coconut mixture.

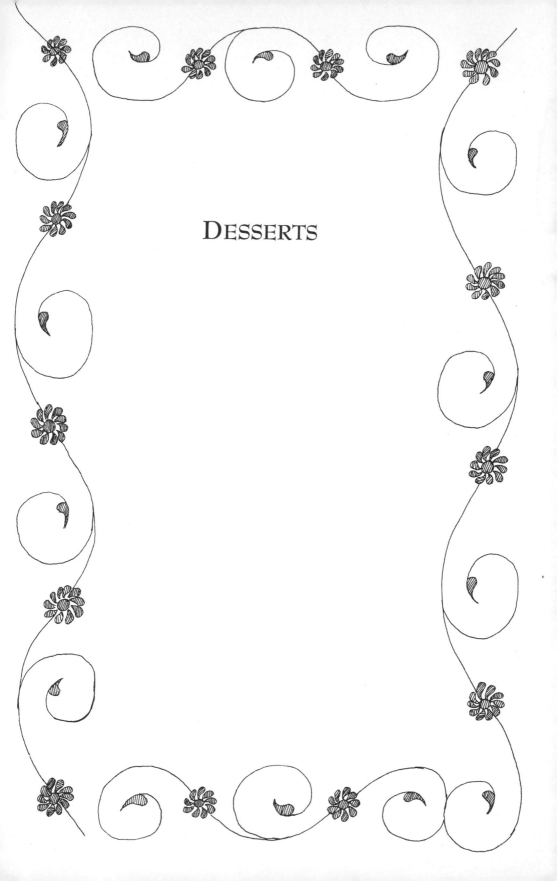

DESSERTS

GULAB JAMUN

MILK DUMPLINGS IN SYRUP

*U*ndoubtedly the best known Indian sweet is the Bengali gulab jamun, little milk dumplings based on milk powder which are deep-fried and soaked in rose-flavoured syrup spiced with cardamom. The way to success lies in the milk powder and there are two alternatives. Go to an Indian speciality shop and ask for a packet of full cream milk powder for gulab jamun. Otherwise settle for the next best thing: St Ivel Five Pints which makes an acceptable substitute and was recommended to me by Indian home cooks. Don't use baby formulas or any other dried milks as they could let you down.

Serves 4–6

DUMPLINGS:		
75 g	full cream milk powder	3 oz/¾ cup
45 ml	plain (all-purpose) flour	3 tbsp
2.5 ml	baking powder	½ tsp
25 g	butter, at room temperature	1 oz/2 tbsp
60 ml	cold water	4 tbsp
	Oil for deep-frying	

SYRUP:		
100 g	golden (corn) syrup	4 oz/½ cup
150 ml	hot water	¼ pt/⅔ cup
	Seeds from 6 green cardamom pods	
15 ml	rose water	1 tbsp

1. Sift the milk powder into a bowl with the flour and baking powder.

2. Rub in the butter finely then mix to a stiff and rocky-looking dough with the water.

3. Roll smoothly into 12 even-sized dumplings with slightly dampened hands then deep-fry for 3–4 minutes in hot oil until they swell to double their original size.

4. Turn over several times with a wooden spoon, remove from the pan and drain on crumpled kitchen paper.

5. For the syrup, put the golden syrup, water and cardamom pods into a pan and bring to the boil, stirring. Add the rose water and pour into a dish.

6. Add the dumplings one by one and leave to soak until just cold. Serve in twos in small dishes, coating with the syrup.

MANGO KULFI

MANGO ICE CREAM

*M*aking ice cream in northern India is a big production so I
have by-passed the more time-consuming elements and come
up with an alternative which is much quicker to make. Restaurant kulfi
is frozen in special cone-shaped moulds but at home, use a bowl and
scoop portions on to plates. Garnish with a sprinkling of chopped
pistachio nuts.

Serves 6–8

	2 large and fairly ripe mangoes	
425 g	OR canned mango	15 oz/2 cups
	slices in syrup	
400 g	canned sweetened	14 oz/1 cup
	condensed milk	
	Seeds from 4 green cardamom pods	
30 ml	finely chopped pistachio nuts	2 tbsp

1. Peel the mangoes then cut the flesh away from the large,
central and flattish stones. Blend to a smooth purée in a blender or food
processor. Alternatively, do the same thing with the canned mangoes
and syrup.

2. Transfer to a bowl then gently whisk in the condensed
milk. Stir in the cardamom seeds.

3. Cover and freeze for 2 hours. Whisk until smooth then re-
cover and freeze until firm, allowing at least 3–4 hours.

4. Soften slightly before serving, scoop into dishes and
sprinkle each one with chopped pistachios.

SEVIYAN KHEER

VERMICELLI MILK PUDDING

A lavish and luxurious rose-perfumed milk pudding from the Punjab based on butter-fried vermicelli, flaked almonds and milk. Some serve it warm, others lightly chilled and either way it's quite stunning with its topping of cream and vivid green chopped pistachios. Serves 8

45 g	butter, ghee or clarified butter	1½ oz/3 tbsp
75 g	vermicelli, coarsely crushed	3 oz/3 cups
50 g	flaked almonds	2 oz/¾ cup
1.2 l	full cream milk	2 pts/5 cups
45 ml	caster sugar	3 tbsp
45 ml	rose water	3 tbsp
40 ml	thick (heavy) cream	8 tsp
40 ml	chopped pistachio nuts	8 tsp

1. Melt the butter in a fairly large saucepan. Add the vermicelli and fry slowly, stirring frequently, until it turns light golden brown. This can take up to about 10 minutes.

2. Mix in the almonds and continue to fry for 1–2 minutes until they turn pale gold.

3. Gradually pour in the milk and bring slowly to the boil, stirring all the time. Lower the heat, two-thirds cover the pan with a lid and simmer for 25 minutes.

4. Stir in the sugar and rose water. Divide equally between 8 serving bowls and serve warm or just cold, each topped with cream and pistachios.

KHEER

RICE PUDDING

*U*nlike any other rice pudding, the kheer is soft and camelia-coloured, not too sweet, dotted with sultanas and, like so many oriental puddings, scented with rose water. This one is from northern India.

Serves 6

1.2 l	full cream milk	2 pts/5 cups
175 g	short-grain rice	6 oz/1 cup
	Seeds from 4 cardamom pods	
60 ml	sugar	4 tbsp
30 ml	sultanas (golden raisins)	2 tbsp
30 ml	rose water	2 tbsp

1. Put all the ingredients except the rose water into a large, heavy-based pan. Bring to the boil, stirring.

2. Lower the heat, leave uncovered and simmer very gently for about 50 minutes, stirring often to prevent the mixture from sticking and catching.

3. Add rose water, spoon into dishes and serve warm.

FIRNI

RICE CREAM

A cooling rice cream from the north, brilliantly white, this is quick to make and delicately cooling. It could be likened to a thin version of blancmange and Indians sometimes eat it at the beginning of the meal.

Serves 6

75 ml	rice flour	5 tbsp
45 ml	cold water	3 tbsp
900 ml	cold milk	1½ pts/3¾ cups
100 g	sugar	4 oz/½ cup
30 ml	rose water	2 tbsp
15 ml	blanched and chopped toasted almonds	1 tbsp
15 ml	chopped pistachio nuts	1 tbsp

1. Blend the rice flour to a thinnish cream by adding gradual amounts of cold water.

2. Heat the milk slowly until hot in a saucepan. Add about a quarter to the blended rice flour, mixing thoroughly. Return to the pan.

3. Cook, stirring constantly, until the mixture comes to the boil and thickens slightly.

4. Add the sugar then lower the heat and simmer for 8 minutes, stirring from time to time. Cool slightly and blend in the rose water.

5. Pour into 6 dessert dishes and refrigerate when cold. Before serving, sprinkle chopped nuts over each.

SHRIKHAND

YOGHURT AND SAFFRON DESSERT

ight and creamy in texture and coloured warm yellow, shrikhand, from the west, is one of India's most exquisite desserts and its looks and creamy taste belie the simple ingredients which go into its making. It is usually served in small dishes and often to be found on a thali.

Serves 8

VERSION 1

2.5 ml	saffron strands	½ tsp
15 ml	boiling water	1 tbsp
600 ml	thick yoghurt	1 pt/2½ cups
	or curd cheese	
175 g	caster (superfine) sugar	6 oz/¾ cup
	2 large pinches of grated nutmeg	
40 ml	chopped pistachio nuts	8 tsp

1. Soak the saffron in the boiling water for 30 minutes.

2. Tip the yoghurt or curd cheese into a bowl. Add the sugar, nutmeg and saffron with the water in which it was soaked.

3. Stir fairly briskly until evenly combined then spoon equal amounts into 8 ramekin dishes. Chill lightly and sprinkle with nuts just before serving.

VERSION 2

Follow the recipe above, using fromage frais instead of the yoghurt. Also include 150 ml/¼ pt/⅔ cup extra thick double cream (heavy cream) and reduce the sugar by 25 g/1 oz/2 tsp as the fromage frais and cream combined have a sweetish after-taste.

TAMATTAR BARFI

TOMATO FUDGE

he sweetest of sweets (candy) served throughout India, this is something like a sugary fudge and different enough to make everybody I know who's tried it ask for the recipe.
   Serves 8–10

450 g	tomatoes, skinned and chopped	1 lb
150 g	granulated sugar	5 oz/⅔ cup
150 ml	water	¼ pt/⅔ cup
175 g	desiccated (shredded) coconut	6 oz/2 cups
Seeds from 5 green cardamom pods		

1. Lightly grease a 15 cm/6 in square dish.

2. Put all the ingredients into a saucepan. Stir over a low heat until sugar completely dissolves.

3. Bring to the boil, stirring. Lower the heat slightly and continue to boil until the fudge glistens, looks fairly thick and comes cleanly away from the sides of the pan. Stir almost constantly.

4. Stand the pan in a sink one-third filled with cold water and beat steadily until the fudge becomes almost solid.

5. Spread into the prepared dish with a knife dipped in and out of hot water. Leave until firm and cold before cutting into cubes.

PANCHAMRITAM

FRUITED BANANA DESSERT

lmost chocolate brown in colour and exceptionally sweet, this southern dessert is an amazing venture into the unknown and well worth the journey.

Serves 8

30 ml	raisins	2 tbsp
	Boiling water	
	4 medium bananas, fully ripe	
30 ml	finely chopped dates	2 tbsp
1.5 ml	ground cardamom	¼ tsp
2.5 ml	ground ginger	½ tsp
2.5 ml	cinnamon	½ tsp
100 g	dark brown molasses sugar	4 oz/½ cup

1. Soak the raisins in boiling water to cover. Drain.

2. Finely mash the bananas then stir in raisins and all the remaining ingredients.

3. Cover and chill lightly before serving, keeping portions small.

Gajar Ka Halwa

CARROT PUDDING

*U*nique by any standards, this particular pudding is a blissful dessert based on carrots and milk with a background of cardamom. It's served in the best restaurants, in the best homes, a family tradition in the Punjab, a comfortable indulgence. The recipe below, many generations old, has come to me directly from a dear friend in India and is an outstanding contribution.

Serves 8–10

1 kg	carrots, grated	2 lb
300 ml	boiling water	½ pt/1¼ cups
1 l	full cream milk	1¾ pts/4¼ cups
75 ml	caster (superfine) sugar	5 tbsp
25 g	unsalted butter	1 oz/2 tbsp
	Seeds from 6 cardamom pods	
45 ml	raisins	3 tbsp
45 ml	blanched and chopped almonds	3 tbsp
45 ml	chopped pistachio nuts	3 tbsp

1. Put the carrots into a roomy saucepan with the boiling water. Boil for 5 minutes.

2. Pour in the milk then simmer 1–1½ hours until virtually all the liquid has been absorbed by the carrots. Stir frequently.

3. Mix in the sugar and simmer for 10 minutes, stirring all the time.

4. Add the butter, cardamom seeds, raisins and half the nuts. Spoon into dessert bowls, sprinkle with remaining nuts and serve warm.

DRINKS

MASALA CHAI

SPICED TEA

*T*he first time I tasted spiced tea was at an Indian friend's home in north London. It was rich, milky, sweet and fragrant and an unexpected pleasure.

Serves 4-6

	8 green cardamom pods	
2.5 cm	cinnamon stick	1 in
	3 black peppercorns	
	3 tea bags	
450 ml	boiling water	¾ pt/2 cups
450 ml	milk	¾ pt/2 cups
20 ml	sugar or sugar substitute	4 tsp

1. Bruise the cardamom pods by tapping with a hammer until they split slightly.

2. Put into a saucepan with remaining ingredients. Bring to the boil and simmer for 4 minutes. Strain into cups and drink hot.

LASSI

YOGHURT DRINK

assi is probably the national drink of India, a light and tangy yoghurt froth which goes perfectly with curries or any other type of Indian meal. It can be sweet or savoury, is much favoured by vegetarians or those not permitted to drink alcohol and should be slightly foamy, therefore best made in a blender.

Serves about 6

300 ml	thick yoghurt	½ pt/1¼ cups
900 ml	chilled water	1½ pt/3¾ cups
10 ml	salt	2 tsp
Chopped fresh coriander (cilantro)		
Ground cumin		

1. Scrape the yoghurt into a blender and whizz with half the water until frothy.

2. Transfer to a large jug and gradually whisk in rest of the water and the salt.

3. Pour into tumblers and sprinkle with the chopped coriander and the cumin.

For sweet Lassi:
Add a few teaspoons sugar instead of the salt and sprinkle only with cumin or a little garam masala.

ACKNOWLEDGEMENTS

Personal

My love, memories and thanks always to:

The kind, gentle and gracious Indians who befriended me when I was a small child living in the bewildering and unfamiliar scenario of Africa and gave me the freedom to explore their own fragrant world of herbs, spices, magical sweetmeats and exotic fruits.

My late Uncle Mike, a lover of life and beloved relative, who introduced me to gourmet pleasures at the age of three when he sat me in a high chair in London's Cumberland Hotel and fed me Knickerbocker Glories not much smaller than me. Later on, we progressed to his favourite Veeraswamy's restaurant where we feasted on the finest and where the magnificent food was my first introduction to the joys of Indian cuisine.

My dear Anglo-Indian friend Tessa, whose parents and three brothers 'adopted' me as a kind of family pet and let me share their lives for so many happy years. What wonderful times we had in the kitchen watching mother cook and how lucky I was, in my formative years, to be taken out to eat with them in carefully chosen Indian restaurants whenever there was occasion to celebrate.

Companies

Thank you to the following for supplying ingredients for some of the recipes in the book and also for giving information:

Schwarz and Sharwoods – herbs and spices
Veetee – rice
Nestlé – instant coconut milk powder
Dufrais – oils and vinegars
Geeta – chutneys and pickles
Tate & Lyle – sugars

Equipment

Kenwood – juice extractor
Magimix – food processor accessories

Restaurants:

For supplying menus
Diwana Bhel-Poori House in Drummond Street, close to
London's Euston
Chutneys
Ravi Shankar vegetarian restaurants, also in Drummond
Street
Surya Vegetarian restaurant, West Hampstead, London
St James Court, St James, London
Hare Krishna vegetarian restaurant, Tottenham Court Road,
London
Vijay, Willesden, London
Sundarban Tandoori, Cricklewood, London
Gulshan Tandoori, Harrow, Middlesex
Curry Centre, Edgware, Middlesex
Karahi King, North Wembley, Middlesex
Jaipur Tandoori, Watford, Hertfordshire
Lal Bagh Tandoori, Bushey, Hertfordshire
India Garden Tandoori, Bushey, Hertfordshire
Sonargoan, Bushey Heath, Hertfordshire
Jamuna, Bath, Avon
The Spice of Life, Isle of Man
The Sultan of Lancaster, Lancaster
The Bombay, Lancaster
Al-Sheikh's, Stoke-on-Trent
Jamals Tandoori, Oxford
The Mirabai, Oxford
The Standard, Oxford

And other restaurants in the North Country, Lake District, Scotland, Kent, the West Country and further afield in South Africa and USA.

My appreciation for their time and help to:
Anne Birnhak of Press Gang and the management of St James Court in London for inviting us to their glittering and sumptuous Indian festival dinners.

The owners of The Sultan of Lancaster who have transformed a run down Methodist Church in the city centre into one of the most truly beautiful and exciting restaurants in England by virtue of decor and fine food.

Diwana, one of my favourite Indian restaurants in London, for always providing consistently good and genuine food and multi-fashioned pancakes (dosas) which are a triumph of culinary skill.

The husband and wife team, Adi and Azra Adi, of the Karahi restaurant in Wembley, for allowing me hours of study behind the scenes.

INDEX

Page numbers in *italics* refer to menu descriptions